Christoffe

Relationships?

WHICH BRAIN IS TALKING?

The ultimate guide to happy,
healthy & successful relationships.

For more information on training, development, and coaching for Three Brains Leadership whole leadership go to Christoffel Sneijders website at 3brainsacademy.com

Get your personal Three Brains Preference Assessment at 3BrainsAssesment.com

Email Christoffel Sneijders at christoffel@3brainsacademy.com

TABLE OF CONTENTS

Introduction: Love and relationships are better
using your Three Brains   9

Why is it so hard to understand the other...
from divorce(s) to inspiration   14

Do we really have Three Brains, a Head Brain,
a Heart Brain and a Gut Brain?   16

**SECTION 1: WHY YOUR THREE BRAINS ARE BOTH THE
SOLUTION AND PROBLEM FOR EVERY GREAT RELATIONSHIP?**   21

1. Harmony: Three happy Brains is our default programming   23

When your Brains agree...happiness is in your reach   26

When our Three Brains disagree... all relationships go downhill   27

2. What are the Five reasons we don't have
our Three Brains aligned?   31

Reason one: We misunderstand how our mind
(one vs Three Brains) really works   32

Reason two: Our Gut and Heart Brains disagree
about 'Me' and 'Us' when making decisions   34

Reason three: Most societies and cultures cultivate Gut Brain behavior   36

Reason four: Gender stereotypes:
The hoax of feminine and masculine traits   40

Socialization and stereotyping   42
The myth and bad science of gender-linked inherent abilities   46

Reason five: We underestimate the power that trauma,
abuse or bullying have on our Three Brains   48

A traumatized Gut Brain is like a bull in a China shop   53

Abuse: The most damaging trauma of all for our relationships   56

The poison of a traumatized Heart — betrayal, grief, and bullying   60

     Betrayal   60

     Grief   61

     Bullying and the devastating scars they can leave behind   65

The traumatized Head Brain — when logic fails, what is left?   66

Mental illness makes lovers into both therapists and clients   70

SECTION 2: WHAT IS YOUR DOMINANT BRAIN?   75

3. Who is your boss? Your Head, Your Heart or Your Gut?   77

4. Do the free Three Brains Preference
Assessment to have your insight in how your Brains decide   81

5. Our Three Brains' strengths and weaknesses   83

    The Gut Brain's strength — the watchdog, 'Me' first   83

    The Gut Brain's weakness — a blunt instrument   85

    The Heart Brain's strengths — loving, caring and courageous   86

    The Heart Brain's weaknesses — naïve, trusting and self-sacrificing   87

    The Head Brain's strength — logic, knowledge and creativity   88

    The Head Brain's weakness — emotionally incompetent   90

6. How our Brains learn, decides how we act   93

SECTION 3: WHAT ARE PROS AND CONS OF A HEAD,
HEART AND GUT BRAIN PARTNER?   101

7. Gut Brain Partners: achievers, competitors,
action oriented, and not the best for long lasting relationships   103

    The good things about the Gut Brain (because it is an amazing Brain)   103

    The Gut Brain's main objective is the opposite of a healthy relationship   107

Desire and lust, without them there is no life   111

In Survival mode there is no time for relationships   114

Rage is so useful until it is not   116

The beauty of Hunger and disgust   117

Gut Brain domination: Run, fight or freeze   124

Should You Avoid Gut Brain People Altogether?   125

8. Heart Brain partners: connecting, loyal, self-sacrificing and it is always about "us"   131

Heart Brain emotions, the connection builders   132

Heart Brain people they have a tendency for trying to heal damaged people … to their own detriment   136

Heart Brain people are the team builders   139

Heart Brain people are the courageous ones   139

Why do we hate? And why is it healthy to do so?   141

Heart Brain domination: The love factor   143

9. Head Brain Partners: logical, Rational, and as long it makes sense all is good   145

Does the Head Brain Partner have emotions? Do logical emotions exist?   148

How does the Head Brain express thoughts as "emotions"?   154

Head Brain domination: Let's puzzle this out   157

10. Is it love or sex with your Three Brains?   161

How do our Three Brains address sex or lovemaking differently?   163

Gut Brain means sex   164

Gut and Heart Brain is sex/lovemaking   164

SECTION 4: HOW TO DEAL WITH THE HEAD, HEART OR GUT BRAIN PARTNERS? THE KEY: WHICH BRAIN IS TALKING? 167

11. How do your Brains talk to you? 169
Exercise: Listening to your own Three Brains language 169

12. How to find out: which Brain is talking?
The language and words of our Three Brains 173
Gut Brain words 175
Heart Brain words 175
Disconnecting 176
Head Brain words 176
Three Brains word disasters 179

13. Partnership: What are the Two magic bullets? 181
Magic bullet 1: 183
Magic bullet 2: 184

14. How to engage with the Head,
Heart and Gut Brain, the eighteen golden rules 185
The 8 rules of dealing with Gut Brain dominated people 186
The four rules of dealing with Head Brains: understand before being understood 203
The six rules of dealing with Heart Brains: stay connected 208

15. The seven essential steps to really connect with the other person 213

SECTION 5: FOR WHEN YOU HAVE CHILDREN, HOW DO THEIR THREE BRAINS WORK? 225

16. Children also have Three Brains
(But only two are booted up) 227
17. The first two years 233

18. Ages two through five   243

19. The pre-teen years, from two to Three Brains   251

20. Teenagers, Three Brains struggling for control   255

    Risk-taking is a risk for teenagers   257

    How to defang a teenager's Gut Brain   258

21. Children and divorce, consistency and honesty is the key   263

SECTION 6: FOR ALL THE NERDIES LIKE ME, THREE BRAIN SCIENCE   267

22. The science behind our Three Brains   269

    Scientific proof of the Three Brains   269

    Evolution of our Three Brains   275

23. Makeup of our Three Brains and how they are connected   281

    Autonomic nervous system   283

    Parasympathetic nervous system and the Cranial X, the magic one's   285

24. Other methods of communication, light, & energy   295

25. Recap, last words and a request   303

Acknowledgements   305

About Christoffel   309

Sources and notes   311

Introduction:

LOVE AND RELATIONSHIPS ARE BETTER USING YOUR THREE BRAINS

I have had it with you and us, I would rather be alone than with someone like you. Those words kept ringing in his ears.

He did not see this coming; he knew that she had been acting less enthusiastically and affectionate towards him but he thought this was the result of all their recent promotions and increased work commitments. Working from home is hard as the work/life balance becomes really fuzzy. The constant challenge is how to establish the boundaries? He was paying attention to his health and fitness. He had a great well paid job which afforded them an affluent lifestyle with frequent holidays and a beautiful car

The more he thought about it, the more he could not understand what had gone wrong?

She could still feel the sensations in her heart and the crispy feeling in her gut when she thought about her last words to him:

"I need to be with someone who I can connect with on an emotional level and not only on a transactional level."

It was hard and she felt she deserved more than being together with the typical alpha male guy. Although he was good looking, had a good job, and was intelligent, she never really knew how he felt as he always hid his true feelings.

I wonder, how many times have you been in a situation or conversation with a partner or loved one, and felt that you just couldn't get through to them? You both understood the words, but neither of you were hearing the other? Like you were both communicating on different wave lengths. It's frustrating and disappointing but it happens all the time.

How many times, after a conflict, disagreement or a break-up would you have loved to have known what was happening and why, earlier? Why you stayed in that relationship although there were signs that you did not pick up on? Why did you not communicate better?

Why is it so hard to have happy relationships? You would think that cutting-edge science would not be needed to address this question. After millions of years of evolution you'd think we'd have worked out by now how to understand, get along with one another, and connect or fall in love with the right partner.

So many guru's, philosophers and poets have shared many insights, but none of them give real answers to this question. As a therapist, coach, and associate professor of the science of behavioral organizational leadership and communication, I have always wondered what we have unlearned over the years, or what have we learned that is not actually true?

Why do we fall for the bad boy or girl, why do we want to rescue them? Why is it hard to share our emotions? Why is it sometimes so hard to be vulnerable and why do people say the things they do?

What is the connection between that gut-wrenching or passionate feeling in our heart, and our communications and interactions? And how can science have proven we react to stimuli seconds before we are consciously aware of them? Who is in charge inside us?[1]

When you talk to someone — even your partner — do you really understand their intended meaning? Is it clear to you what they want to get out of the conversation? Is it actually really clear what you want? Moreover, is there a shared understanding of where this interaction fits in the context of your relationship?

When you look at the science, you realize that human beings, the greatest thinking machines that have ever existed on this planet, don't have much insight into how their own thinking processes work, how emotions are made and that they run the show.

In the absence of a real grasp of what makes ourselves and others tick, we have been treated to one 'theory of the mind' after another. Some theories claim to be scientific — based on observations and case studies. Others are metaphysical or philosophical — based on thinking deeply about people and humanity. Still more have been made up by well-meaning people or by charlatans out to make a quick buck. The shelves of bookstore self-help sections groan under their weight with each peddling one vapid insight after another.

This book, which is a revised and updated version of my previous book "how men and women fit, finally understand you partner with the Three Brains theory" is built around crucial new insights into the science of human thinking and feeling. Current research has upended the notion that we have in our heads a single powerful mind that is home to our thoughts, emotions, and reactions. In fact, science now tells us that we have not one, but **three** centers of thought, memory and decision-making! Although we all perceive, interpret, and react to the world in a distinctly different way, those 3 centers of wisdom have the same base drivers.

It is "just" the combination that makes it difficult and the fact that we actually do not know that we have these 3 centers of wisdom. Up to now we shared this as: we have conscious awareness (or mind) and an unconscious awareness (or mind) and that unconsciousness mind is responsible for 90% of our behaviors and actions. As it is unconscious, we try our best to influence it with our conscious mind. Like a blind person trying to find his way in unknown city.

> In addition to our well-known 'thinking' brain (which I will call the 'Head Brain'), we have a 'relationship' brain (which I will call our 'Heart Brain') and a third brain — at our core — whose job it is to keep us safe. I will call this 'self-preservation' brain the 'Gut Brain'.

When we get angry or upset, what triggers those feelings and emotions?

If the Head Brain (or the limbic, or cerebellum brain) was truly the only home to our thoughts and feelings, why is it so hard to talk ourselves out of feelings and emotions?

When we feel bad, where do we feel bad? In our Head, in our Heart or in our Gut?

When our hearts are broken or our guts are churning with anxiety, why is it that the dispassionately rational thoughts in our heads don't make a dent in our emotions?

When we're inclined to blurt out things, we know we shouldn't say, what compels us to do it anyway?

My clients, my coachees, or the people I meet, often try to explain that any shared understanding with their partner, children, parents or colleagues is next to impossible; especially when that interaction is with someone with a different gender. They tell me "You know men are from Mars and women are from Venus" meaning that it is obvious we speak different emotional languages.

We have come, in part thanks to that popular book of John Gray and its ubiquitous metaphor that many took too literally, to take as a revealed truth that such misunderstandings are a natural result of ingrained gender differences. *Nonsense. Or let me put it more clearly: NONSENSE!* That was never what John wanted as the main take away. Yes, we are biologically different and that not does not mean we are have to be different.

Men, women or whatever your gender is, do not come from different planets. We are all human. But being human is a complicated thing. It's hard enough to understand what drives our own thinking and ways of communicating, much less interpret what someone who was raised and socialized differently is really meaning or thinking, when they may not even know themselves. The fact that men and women have a tough time fitting in with one another is no surprise when you broaden the picture to understand that people have trouble fitting in with other people! Gender is only one factor, there are many, many others. In this book, the gender of you or your partner doesn't matter. The insights and skills we develop will enhance each one of our relationships.

Now is the time to use that knowledge to solve the problems of our own relationships, and find happiness.

Why is it so hard to understand the other... from divorce(s) to inspiration

The longer I worked as a therapist and coach, the more I felt that something was missing — I didn't know what — in my understanding of how people were applying the insights I was helping them towards. Were the solutions we found to people's problems in my office leading to better lives in the real world? Sometimes, it seemed not. Making an intellectual breakthrough was one thing. But true emotional healing and personal change were altogether different. Understanding did not always lead to healing.

The less I followed my logical thoughts in working with someone, and the more I followed my 'instinct', the more success I had. It did not make logical sense, even though the results showed it was the right path.

Sometimes, I observed that the behavioral changes I expected to flow from intellectual and emotional understandings were not happening. Other times, people who seemed immune to insight suddenly improved anyway.

It is a crisis of purpose and practice faced by many people in my field. You do the demanding work of verbalizing an issue or emotional malfunction and then... Nothing much changes. Unhealthy or destructive patterns persist. As the French would put it, "Plus ça change, plus c'est la même chose". For many of my patients, it was painfully true that "the more things changed, the more they stayed the same".

My life is no exception. Many people have an incident in their life that inspires them to do things that they had never thought possible. In my case, writing this book was not something I would ever have envisioned. Finding that I had something to say came to me gradually over time, after hitting a brick wall after my third divorce.

I forced myself to REthink and REfeel everything I knew and experienced regarding relationships and personal heartbreak. The shock, depression, grief, and self-blame did not grow easier to bear with the experience of having failed again and again. I was repeatedly doing the same thing, hoping for a different result.

So, I took a deep dive to understand why I messed up in my own divorces (yes plural) and relationships–was it because I was bullied at school and carried for a long time trust issues with me, or were there other hidden factors playing a role?–and did my best to distinguish between the reasons we make the decisions we do, and why we communicate (or not) the way we do.

I came to feel and understand that there was much more going on than could be explained by my traditional training. It took me a long time to piece together what was really happening inside my own mind and that of my patients and coachees. I spent a lot of time thinking, observing, and pouring through the scientific literature in my field and many others. I came to understand that the part of the brain that we are educated to work with, was only part of a much larger picture. That picture has been forming for millions of years, as human beings have evolved the cognitive structures required to survive in the world, to understand it, and to make decisions.

I went back to my 30 years of work experience and searched for new learnings from a different angle. I analyzed my therapy/coaching clients even more than usual.

I started to experiment with connecting concepts and creating new ones in my neuro-linguistic programming (NLP) and clinical hypnotherapy training, and especially in the workshops, 'Awaken and Live your Potential' and 'Connect, Coach and Lead from the Head, Heart and Gut'. This gave me the insights to connect the dots. I built on them and discovered a whole new approach to understanding how people communicate — and fail to communicate and connect — in relationships.

The human brain (the one in our head) is an amazing thing. It's the one reading this page and understanding the words and language, it is an amazing success story in evolutionary history. But it is only the servant of our Heart Brain and Gut Brain. Whatever insecurities you might have, know this: You are evolution's triumph.

How could mere words flitting across the surfaces of our minds ever change anything, when what was really going on was far below the surface?

Before we begin, a couple of notes...

Do we really have Three Brains, a Head Brain, a Heart Brain and a Gut Brain?

Let's be clear at this point: I am not talking in metaphors. This book is not built around some intellectual concept to help us think about how that one brain inside our skull works, that is still described as Three Brains (reptilian, emotional and mammal) as that is the biggest scientifically hoax you can imagine. But about one in our Head, one in our Heart and one in our Gut.

Our Three Brains – Head, Heart and Gut – are real.

There is a great deal of scientific research on the distinct roles, locations, and functions of the three very distinct cognitive structures we carry around in our head and body.

Before now, if Heart and Gut Brains were thought to exist at all, they were considered separate entities that existed and reacted independently and were not capable of communicating or collaborating with one another. We have come to know differently.

If you are interested in the science, I will go into some detail about the science in the closing section of this book. Until then, the important thing is to understand what the Three Brains are, and how they work. We can then apply the insights resulting from the research in practical ways to help us manage (and sometimes control) our own Brains and how we interact with others. Throughout this book, we move forward from scientific fact — that the Head, Heart and Gut Brains exist — to explore the ways we can use that knowledge to improve our Brains' health, our relationships and our lives.

In the past, the Heart and Gut Brains have been neglected (or dismissed) by Western scientific researchers. In therapy and coaching they are often referred to as the 'unconscious mind'; you may have seen those pictures of icebergs, one tiny part above the water (our conscious mind) and 90% beneath the water (the sub- or unconscious). From this moment on, the subconscious is tangible and has a name: Heart and Gut Brain.

Really important is to know that they don't speak the same language as the Head Brain and they have different objectives. Therefore, their decisions can seem illogical. They can be stubborn and, especially to people whose own Head Brains are dominant, like scientific researchers, what the other Brains contribute can be irritating and seem downright stupid.

But know this before you go one step further: Your Heart and Gut Brains are not stupid. Not one bit. Often, they are much more insightful and attuned to our needs than the Head Brain, which can be distracted and beguiled by shiny objects, bad information, and bogus comparisons. The Heart and Gut Brains experience and interpret our internal and external environments in their own ways. They analyze, remember, and make decisions about what we should do, even when it's hard to put those reasons into words. Words are the Head Brain's domain, and if it doesn't understand something, it can't articulate it. But, if we can screw on our Head Brain correctly, and educate it a bit, we can learn to listen to all Three Brains and become wiser and happier in the process.

Our Three Brains run normally on eco mode and it simplifies everything we do

Our Brains love to generalize, place things into categories and based on those generalizations and categories make snap decisions and they do this by default.

Why?

It saves time and energy, and that is rather important as our Three Brains use approximately 35%[2] of our daily energy consumption! Categories are useful when thinking about some things. Look at a restaurant menu, divided into meat, fish, and vegetarian dishes. This makes it easy to see what is on offer. Categories are worse than useless when we are lumping people into categories — be they 'men' and 'women', LGBTQIA+, or some other way of dividing people into subsets of humanity — it is just wrong. It's avoiding the effort of using our head brain to the full by thinking it through and stepping out of our own survival comfort zone.

Yes, it makes it easy to have a general view of a person but it has the same accuracy as saying that lions, puma's, tigers and cats are all cats and have the same behavior, hence we should act in the same way when we encounter by them. .

So, it boggles the mind to see how many relationship guides, including ones that sell millions of copies, fall into using stereotypes — especially ones that ascribe certain ways of thinking or acting to men and women. It is easy to do — not because male Brains and female Brains are fundamentally different — but because, in most parts of the world, boys and girls are socialized differently and taught to value different aspects of themselves. The famous boys should be boys and girls should be girls idea, and the subsequent socialization leads to them later identifying as the stereotypes. When they grow up to become men and women, they often continue to think of themselves as being defined (or constrained) by culturally defined traits supposed to be characteristic of their gender. This is not a good thing, but it is true. When even the people who are the target of a stereotype start to believe it, you have a real problem. This is one reason stereotypes are so hard to eradicate.

One of my hopes for this book is that we can start to break out of stereotypical thinking. I hope the insights we discuss here will help people re-socialize themselves, so that those who have been encouraged to let their Head and Gut Brains dominate, learn to listen to their Heart Brain, while people who have been trained to prioritize what their Heart Brain advises, open up their hearts to some of the wisdom that they have been ignoring in their Head Brain and even more so in their Gut Brain.

However, your own Brains are configured and which is the most dominant in you–more about that in section 2: Who is your Boss, your Heart your Head, or your Gut?–I hope to help you understand more about them, how they work for you and for the people around you and to provide you with techniques to deal with the people in your life. If I (we) succeed, you will become a more centered, happier person, and a better partner in both your personal and professional life.

To achieve this, we must acknowledge that sometimes only one Brain is in charge, while at other times, a combination of two or all Three Brains are involved in decision-making.

With this knowledge, you will be capable of understanding your own mindset and that of your partner, friends, and colleagues. With such a powerful tool at your disposal, you will be able to break free of stereotypes and say goodbye to many misunderstandings in your life.

Client examples

To illustrate the theory and how our Three Brains work and influence our relationships, I use many client cases to illustrate a point. To protect their identity and secondly, to really Illustrate the essence of what is happening with our Three Brains, all of the examples are a construction of two or more similar client cases.

Section 1:

WHY YOUR THREE BRAINS ARE BOTH THE SOLUTION AND PROBLEM FOR EVERY GREAT RELATIONSHIP?

1.

Harmony: Three happy Brains is our default programming

The fundamental purpose of this book is to give you insights into how you can have happy, healthy relationships! For that you will learn essential insights Into how our Three Brains work, what your preferred ways of acting are, and how to identify that in others!

Finding harmony will bring us closer to our goal. This will result in better and more fully considered decisions and communications that will become the foundation of more harmonious relationships and greater personal happiness.

At the beginning of our lives, that balance and happiness came naturally…

Happiness

We are born with happy and healthy Head, Heart and Gut Brains. They are not fully developed, but they are in sync with one another.

If you do not believe me, just watch little babies. They smile, laugh at us, and do their best to connect; they only cry when they need something. And when babies play, they play together, they don't compete with each other.

Now, remember a time when you were simply happy, calm, and relaxed. You may not have understood it at the time, but that was a moment when your Three Brains were in total agreement. Sadly, for most of us, such moments don't come along every day. What was it that created that inner harmony?

So the question is: "Do you need just one of your Brains to be content, or all of them?"

Surprisingly, material success (this is the domain of the Gut Brain)–beyond what is required for a stable, healthy life–is not a significant factor in happiness. According to the World Happiness Report 2018, the USA, the world's most prosperous nation, only ranks 18th out of 156 countries — below most highly-developed nations.[3]

So why is that?

if it's not wealth or material goods, what is the root of personal happiness?

The USA performs poorly on social measures, which is a Heart Brain activity: life expectancy is going down; inequality is up and confidence in the government has fallen. As a result, Americans take more antidepressants than the people of any other nation.[4]

This is a classic example of only one Brain making the decisions. Yes, material success is important as it satisfies the needs of the Gut Brain but it does not fulfil the needs of the Heart Brain, hence a misbalance.

What are we missing?

In his book Happiness and Flourishing, writer Martin Seligman cites five essentials for a flourishing and happy life:[5] and it provides an insight into why we need our Three Brains and not only one

- Positive emotions, these are a result of your Heart Brain with a satisfied Gut Brain
- Engagement is the field of your Heart Brain and Head Brain
- Relationships again this is your Heart Brain competence
- Meaning in life for this we need all 3, our Head, Gut and Heart Brain
- Achievements this is where your Gut Brain is the driving force

Happiness, in essence, is the feeling of being safe in the world and in your relationships. In Brain language, it means our Gut Brain isn't feeling endangered, which frees our Heart Brain to make satisfying emotional connections. Happiness is your natural state when you are safe, and when your basic needs such as food and physical comfort are met. Hence, cared-for babies can be literal 'bundles of joy'. Until they are hungry, uncomfortable, or scared — then they become bundles of something else entirely.

When we look at research worldwide, the people who are most serene live in Panama, Costa Rica, Denmark, Austria, Brazil, Uruguay, Sweden, El Salvador, Sweden, Guatemala, and Canada. So, six of the top ten happiest countries are not even close to being the world's wealthiest.[6]

Can we, as adults, achieve the happiness we felt as children? Of course, we can! And we can do it without reverting to our childhood.

When all Three Brains are aligned and balanced, and there is no domination of one over the other — a state of mindfulness can be achieved — it is the natural state of childhood and adulthood. But to get there, we sometimes need to clear out the things that get in our way.

When your Brains agree...happiness is in your reach

When everything, cerebrally-speaking, is working as it should, our Brains are cooperating — thinking and acting in harmony. Humans are an amazingly complex system that has evolved to work together to keep us alive and healthy. Our Three Brains, with their 100 billion cells and 100 trillion connections, have evolved to work together to keep us safe, secure, and happy. So, when your Three Brains agree, and they are working with each other as one mind, things feel normal. If we are not under stress or facing a big decision, this is the most common state.

When you are working or doing a hobby and having that feeling of flow, when hours seem like minutes, this is also one of those times when your Three Brains are totally aligned in supporting the action, behavior, or communication.

Another example is when you are in a café with a friend (Gut Brain is happy and feels safe), we have something to satisfy our Gut Brain, a coffee/tea and maybe a snack (Gut Brain is happy) and on the Heart level it feels good to be with a friend.

And why is a friend a friend? Because on the connection level (Heart Brain), we share many of the same values. We find support for our issues, no disagreement and someone who is an ally (that is truly satisfying for our Gut Brain).

When you think about those moments when you sit with your partner in a restaurant or at the dinner table, you are comfortably at ease the Gut Brain is feeling safe, and is being nurtured with food and drink. When you look at your partner you feel at the Heart Brain level that connection, your support and love for each other. The logical Head Brain is sharing about work, about the things that happened during the day, and they are all acknowledged without any judgment. Is that not what we are all looking for?

It is the goal of this book to help you make such moments more and more common, until they become the normal fabric of your everyday life.

When our Three Brains disagree... all relationships go downhill

For us to make decisions that reflect what we genuinely want and need, it is essential that all our Brains are part of the discussion. Otherwise, it is like playing soccer with only a defence lined up or only the strikers; you do not have to be a world-renowned coach to understand that no good can come of it.

> *It is part of our 'biological design' that each Brain has its strengths, and each has characteristic blind spots for which the others compensate. It naturally follows that ignoring or suppressing the input of one of our Brains will lead to flawed decisions.*

When it's our Gut Brain that takes control, we will make a decision that is (like the Gut Brain itself) selfish, short-sighted and all for our own good, with a positive intention only for 'Me'. Your Gut Brain will view other people either as supporters or allies, rivals, or neutral. It will ask, "Which of them is kindly disposed to 'me'? Who has the power to help 'me' advance or succeed? Who is a rival? Who is a backstabber? Who is neither a threat nor an ally?" We can easily create conflicts and hurt feelings, making future problems for ourselves that a Gut Brain does not envisage. Who cares about paying the bills or even being late with paying your bills when you are running to escape a hungry bear?

If it's the Heart Brain making our decisions, we can easily fall into the trap of making decisions that are good for other people — but not the right one for us. Your Heart Brain will perceive it from the perspective of friendship and teamwork. Who can I connect to? Who do I like? With whom can I cooperate on a task? Or share a lunch? The Heart Brain will always try to steer us to a decision that will be applauded by the people we want to please, regardless of whether we should be attempting to please them at that moment, and with that decision. A Heart Brain, untampered by a Gut Brain's "is this right for me?" filter can turn people into doormats, the pleasers.

A Head Brain making decisions is another matter altogether. Head Brains care little about people — including ourselves. The Head Brain will contribute its own analysis. With whom could you have an in-depth discussion about your work and how you, the team or company, could do it better? What is the best way to approach the job to be done? What skills or knowledge will be required to do it? How long will it take? This works fine if the discussion is limited to engineering, science, or accounting. But making a decision based entirely on what seems logical or reasonable, oblivious to any consideration of what is the right decision for us or the people we care about, can put us on the road to heartbreak just as quickly as a Gut Brain's selfishness.

You could ask the same questions about your friends. Which of your friends really has your best interests at heart and do you feel safe with? (Gut Brain) Which of your friends do you feel connected to? (Heart Brain) And with which of them could you really have an interesting and productive conversation? (Head Brain)

Can you see how each of our Three Brains connect in different ways, even to the people closest to us?

Why would your Head Brain keep you awake during the night, rethinking the argument, finding reasons to explain why it happened? It knows you need to sleep, yet still overrules the signals of falling asleep.

The Head Brain can only do that if it is supported by the Gut Brain or Heart Brain. The Gut Brain is not satisfied with the conflict and the solution, furthermore it does not feel safe, or still feels angry, and likes to have a smart way to deal with it. So, it activates the sympathetic nerve (fight or flight) and keeps you awake.

Even when your Heart is broken, the Gut will get activated, even if it is slight ("Why does the Heart feel pain?" it will ask, "Is safety at risk?"). It is up to the Head to find solutions. If your Heart feels disconnected from another person, it could, and most likely will, activate the Gut Brain ("I am left alone."), just like with grief, or when we lose someone or something.

That is why our Brains are meant to interact and to make decisions that respect the perspective of each. It's important to note here that we are not talking about giving any one Brain veto power over a decision — that would just be a different version of One-Brain decision-making. But each of our different viewpoints need to be understood and respected, regardless of what decision is arrived at. The making of such considered decisions is our goal here, and the ticket to continued intra-cranial harmony.

Your Gut Brain in action: having a coffee at the café with a friend

You are sitting in a café with a friend. There are no other people in the café. You feel at ease. Your Gut Brain relaxes and allows the Heart Brain to connect. You start talking about a personal and sensitive work topic. This is something you've been thinking about, so your Head Brain supplies the details and analysis.

Then an unknown person enters the almost empty café. He settles at the table next and close to you.

For at least a second, your Gut Brain will step in and disconnect from your friend. It needs to know whether it is safe to have this discussion within earshot of someone else.

Only when the Gut Brain (after checking the Head Brain to see if it recognizes the person) gives the go-ahead, can we can reconnect and continue with the conversation.

2.

What are the Five reasons we don't have our Three Brains aligned?

There are two fundamental things that form the bedrock of all approaches to improving our lives and our relationships.

One is understanding how we think and feel.

The second is observing and empathizing with others, so that we can understand how they think and feel.

Unless we can grasp the processes within ourselves that are blocking us from thinking/feeling clearly and making good decisions, we cannot change them. With luck and patience, we can sometimes also use our insights to help others or provide a model for them to follow.

Understanding how our Three Brains work is the most important part of any quest for emotional connection and happiness. Until recently, the way we thought about thinking was misguided. We focused almost entirely on the talkative, intelligent, and reasoning parts of our thinking process: our 'Talking Head'. We have ignored, or misunderstood, what goes on beneath the surface. We have overlooked the true power of the parts of our Three Brains that (mostly wordlessly) feel, remember, think, react and, yes, control our decisions and our actions. We have not understood how our Three Brains work. We know, often to our sorrow, that without this understanding, finding happiness, and creating satisfying relationships is much more difficult.

Reading this book and understanding the cutting-edge science behind the insights and techniques introduced cannot, of course, magically solve anyone's relationship issues. But it will equip you with a new understanding that will make you much more likely to succeed.

In short, I aim to make you a happier person and help you create more stable and satisfying emotional relationships.

So why have therapies and self-help gurus gone wrong up to now? There are five main reasons.

Reason one: We misunderstand how our mind (one vs Three Brains) really works

In modern times, we have come to view the human mind as a singular thing. We tend to believe that all our thoughts, feelings and reactions to the world are controlled by a powerful computer in our heads. It is easy to understand how this has happened. It looks like a combined brain, the big blob of gray matter, the limbic mammal emotional brain and the reptilian cerebellum lodged inside our skulls. But, just as your lungs, heart, kidneys, liver, pancreas, and a constellation of other organs, are all crammed into the same abdominal cavity, so, too, your cranium houses three distinct thinking machines, two of which are operated by the Brains downstairs. As a matter of scientific fact, the 'one brain' theory is fundamentally wrong.

In one way, it is another example of how we have ignored or forgotten insights from the past. A few thousand years ago, the Egyptians believed that the heart, rather than the head, was the source of human wisdom.

The heart was, in their view, the center of our emotions, memory, soul, and personality.

In Hinduism the heart has a great significance both as a place where the soul rests and as a representative location of the abode of Brahman. It is the hub and the center of life.

In Buddhism, it is explicit that the heart is the center of wisdom.

In the Bible, we can find many references to the Heart Brain or the lust part of the Gut Brain: Matthew 12:34 "You brood of vipers, how can you who are evil say anything good? For out of the overflow of the heart the mouth speaks." Or in Ephesians 4:17-19 (17) "So I tell you this, and insist on it in the Lord, that you must no longer live as the Gentiles do, in the futility of their thinking."(18) "They are darkened in their understanding and separated from the life of God because of the ignorance that is in them due to the hardening of their hearts."

In fact, as mentioned above, we have three distinct thinking centers (for simplicity's sake, we will call them 'Brains', collectively we will call them your 'Mind'. Each of our Three Brains evolved at different times for different reasons and each perceives, understands, and reacts to the world in its own unique way.

How our Three Brains combination thinks and interacts differs dramatically from one person to another. Your setup, background, and experience are different from mine in profound and important ways, although our three distinct Brains have the same basic functions from one person to the next. Just as we are all born with lungs that breathe, legs that walk, noses that run and other bits of anatomical equipment with specific biological jobs, our Three Brains evolved to perform distinct cognitive tasks:

The **Gut Brain** is our oldest brain (500 million years old). It is in charge of our survival and lust for life. It's an amazingly beautiful and egocentric brain, I like to call it the 'Me' brain. It's something we share with every living creature on the planet.

The **Heart Brain**, which we share with all warm blooded animals, is the seat of relationships. Love, compassion, hate — anything we feel for or about other people or things around us flows from the Heart, it is the true 'Us' brain.

The **Head Brain** was the most recent to evolve in its current size and shape. It is unique to (or, at least, uniquely powerful in) human beings. The Head Brain is not what makes us human — that's something that requires all Three Brains — but it is what makes humans unique. The Head Brain is the home of logic, language and learning. It is an enormous database stuffed with all the facts we have learned and things we have experienced. Its job is not to keep us safe, nor to connect us to others — those jobs were already being done quite well by the two Brains we had already. In us humans it has evolved with primarily one objective: to use the past to predict the future! And therefore, become creative and expressive, to plan, to build, to use tools and language.

Reason two: Our Gut and Heart Brains disagree about 'Me' and 'Us' when making decisions

Can you remember that internal discussion: what do I want and how do I please the other? That is when your Heart and Gut Brain disagree.

And whatever you chose you felt guilty, selfish or "shitty" that you did not take care of yourself.

We all have from time to time that internal feeling that can only be explained by knowing that our Heart and Gut Brain have different priorities and objectives.

Actually, all our 3 Bains have different objective and authorities to keep us happy, healthy and safe.

The **Gut Brain:** This is the most primitive and forceful of our Brains. It is the home of our survival instinct and lust for life. Our Gut is driven by fundamental primal feelings like desire, lust, fear, hunger, disgust, and rage. When the Gut Brain is making decisions, our communication and behavior is rooted in those feelings and desires. It is always focused on 'Me', and it only thinks about the here and now. What do I want now? What I need now? When do I need it? Now! Don't expect beautiful cause and effect analysis for your Gut Brain.

The **Heart Brain:** This warm-blooded beating amazingness is the primary home of our relationship drivers. Our feelings of love, guilt, happiness, hope, joy, shame, sorrow, hate and sadness are all rooted here. Because they are all based on connecting, belonging and are all about 'Us', these feelings are essential to forming and sustaining relationships. This Brain can contribute best to our decisions when we feel safe enough to let our guard down and put the Gut Brain at rest.

The **Head Brain:** This level is solely focused on making reasoned decisions for the future, based on acquired knowledge. It deals with intellectual insights such as understanding, anticipation, interest, surprise, and wonder. All those things can influence our decisions. We can only use this Brain when we are feeling safe enough or when it is consulted by the Gut or Heart Brain. It cannot override the Gut Brain in situations that provoke fear. And, as we mentioned above, it has an almost impossible task trying to convince a Heart Brain to change an emotional decision. Did your Head ever succeed in convincing your Heart not to love somebody?

Reason three: Most societies and cultures cultivate Gut Brain behavior

Most of us were raised to conform to rules that govern how people of our gender, educational and economic background and, sometimes, our ethnic or religious background, "should" act and behave.

Most of our schools promote competition, which means training people's Gut Brains to seek to dominate and defeat. The ultimate focus is on 'Me'. It is the rare institution, indeed, that pays attention to the focus of their students' Heart Brain on cooperation, attachment and harmony. And almost every educational institution is proudest of the intellectual power of the Head Brains it turns out — without regard to whether the people who have them can succeed outside of the academy walls — in the world, in business or in their personal relationships.

The world is ruled by the idea that we must have economic growth to survive, and to compete with other countries, any top 20 list of blockbuster movies is dominated with stories about good and bad people, and how we fight and kill others in order to win and conquer.[7]

Think back to your time at school and university. Where was the greatest emphasis placed, and how was your progress graded?

Why do we have a pass-or-fail system, with grading divisions from A to F, or from 10 to 1? Does it really matter if you pass with a 6 or with a 10?

How many times are you asked at work, "What were your scores at school or university?" Do your managers and colleagues care whether you graduated with the highest honors, or just passed by the smallest margin?

With all the sales people, managers and executive-board members I have trained, this topic never came up when we discussed colleagues and their performance. It was always about how they dealt with clients or colleagues. When a sales person gets an order, it is not important if it is done with the most beautifully, eloquently written and illustrated proposal. The question that is asked is, "Did we get it or not?" Pass or Fail!

Side note on this: Some companies rank their salespeople according to the number of sales, awarding them with bonuses, and creating 'salesperson of the week/month' titles. This is an example of Gut Brain leadership. This is not wrong per se, more that it is telling of the style of leadership.

However, during our time at school or university, our performance is too often compared with that of our fellow students with one-tenth of a difference.

I think we can agree that we are educated to compete and to judge; schools are masters in training our Gut Brain.

The number of children and students who feel hesitant in showing their exam results to their parents is significantly large. It causes them stress when they receive a 6, 7 or 8, instead of 9 or 10, and realize that they have moved to the lower end of the class. My son, who is a primary school teacher, told me that one of his students, an eight-year-old girl, was very upset and worried about the government test she had to take the following week. She was afraid of not doing well. She informed my son that her parents would make her study at length for every test. If she did not do well enough, she had to repeat the exercise until she got a perfect score. How will this make her happy later in life? As a therapist and a parent, it makes me want to cry when I picture her as a future client, who suffers with perfectionism and a fear of failure.

The number of children who now have mental issues is severe and shocking.

An estimated 31.9% of adolescents will experience an anxiety disorder in their life.[8]

The workplace as an arena of combat has been accepted as a guiding principle in the corporate world. In most companies, the focus is not only on external competition; internal competition is also seen as a crucial component of overall corporate success. Following this organizational philosophy has led to many offices and commercial establishments becoming miniature versions of Game of Thrones.

Italian political philosopher, Niccolò Machiavelli, captured this view of the world in the advice he put down for the political leaders of his time:

> *"Whether it be better to be loved than feared or feared than loved? It may be answered that one should wish to be both, but, because it is difficult to unite them in one person, it is much safer to be feared than loved, when, of the two, either must be dispensed with … for love is preserved by the link of obligation which, owing to the baseness of men, is broken at every opportunity for their advantage; but fear preserves you by a dread of punishment which never fails."[9]*

In recent decades, however, the notion that workplaces are most effective when people in them compete with one another has been debunked. Most coaching and training for today's managers and corporate leaders is solely focused on developing teamwork, collaboration, and creativity — all things you can only get by convincing the Gut Brain that it is safe and doesn't need to defeat anyone. The most effective managers, we now know, are the ones who care for and nurture their teams, and who have developed Heart Brains.

That same point is brought home in the book, Trillion Dollar Coach, about Bill Campbell, who helped guide the growth of Google, Apple, and Intuit, amongst many other successful companies. Campbell saw that the formation of trusting relationships, built on teams that felt safe to be creative, was the key to the success of those enterprises. When you foster personal growth and inspire courage (Heart Brain), difficult problems get solved.[10]

Still, it is a sad fact that, even in what we like to think of as a more enlightened time, men are still encouraged to constantly compete, while women feel unrelenting pressure to sacrifice their own goals in order to smooth the troubled waters of the fractious world. Such social pressures are impossible to ignore, difficult to escape and create minefields of miscommunication for people who want to both be themselves and harmonize with others.

One of the most important things we can do, to become more successful in our relationships and in life, is to unlearn some of the things we were raised to accept as natural and true. You know when great thinkers from Steinem to Yoda all agree, they must be onto something:

> The first problem for all of us, men and women, is not to learn, but to unlearn. (Gloria Steinem)

> You must unlearn what you have learned … You will know [the good from the bad] when you are calm, at peace. Passive. (Yoda)

In fact, for people to truly function as happy, successful, connected human beings, all their Brains need to work together, without just one of them being relied upon as the decision-maker.

Reason four: Gender stereotypes: The hoax of feminine and masculine traits

One stereotype, based on the traditional indoctrination mentioned earlier, is that men and women think in fundamentally different ways and that there are masculine and feminine traits. From time to time, some stereotypes contain a grain of truth — but that tiny mote is wrapped in a giant package of nonsense masquerading as wisdom.

It is true, for example, that men and women who were raised in Western cultures were socialized in reasonably similar ways yet still differ; just think of the differences between Scandinavia and the USA. When you travel around the world, you will become aware that men and women communicate, act, and behave differently in different societies based on their socialization. We can call this simple, but appealing myth, **The Masculine/ Feminine Fallacy.**

In fact, the differences from one individual to another in different parts of the world are far greater than those between the male and female genders.

In science, when there is an exception to the facts, it means that "it is not a fact any more but just a hypothesis that is proved wrong"[11]. As not all men and women communicate, act, and behave in the same way, it means it is not a fact or law but just a 'learned' preference.

Still, the myth persists. According to the Masculine/Feminine Fallacy, men are simple creatures, aggressively driven by hormonal urges and desperate for gratification. They think mostly about sex, food, and power so they are solely Gut Brain driven. They will say or do anything to get these things. In this blinkered view, women, driven by a different hormonal mix, are more contextual and emotional in their thinking/feeling processes, focusing on emotional connections, harmony, and security meaning they are only Heart Brain driven.

This simple-minded notion has so infiltrated our popular culture that it now has the status of revealed truth. Take, for instance, the following example: According to Masculine/Feminine thinking, when she says, "Do whatever you want", what she really means is, "Do exactly what I want you to do".

The stereotyped explanation of this is that she knows that she should not and cannot tell her partner what to do. So, she pays lip service to his free will, while also believing that only a dolt would not figure out what she really wants. When you start believing this, you go down the path of believing that women, as a gender, are disingenuous manipulators. And that men, in general, are so far from that sort of behavior that they often can't recognize it when they see it. What a toxic little trap that is to fall into!

Similarly, according to Masculine/Feminine thinking, when she says, "It was a bargain", it's because she doesn't have the courage to confess, "I had to remortgage our house. So please don't ask me how much it cost".

If you start believing this, you could end up thinking that women are compulsive liars, not to mention bubble-headed spendthrifts. Such scenarios make for great sitcom storylines. As a world view however, they leave something to be desired.

Likewise, according to the 'men are Martians' stereotype, men are just as oblique in the way that they express themselves. Accordingly, when he says, "You are overreacting/dramatic", what he is actually doing is blaming a woman for reacting to his bad behavior by asserting that she is emotional (while he, naturally, is the rational one).

Even when he says, "It's my fault, I'm sorry", the Masculine/Feminine approach would decode that into, "We have been arguing about this for hours and I just can't take it anymore. Congratulations, you wore me down. Can we have sex now?"

Again, in this explanation, men are written off as nincompoops who will say anything to end a conflict and satisfy their appetites.

Examples of this sort are entertaining, for sure. As a world view however, they do not pass muster.

If you have fallen into this way of thinking, you will find the creation of satisfying relationships a long journey, indeed. One way to shorten that journey is to keep reading this book.

Socialization and stereotyping

In the Western world today, women are more able than ever to be who they want to be, instead of what society dictates they should be.

As recently as 50 years ago, women were expected to become homemakers and devote their lives to serving their husband and taking care of their children. In short, girls were taught that what mattered about them was how completely they were ruled by their Heart Brains. The idea that they could make their way in the world using the strength of their Head Brains, or that they might follow their Gut Brain's desires was not only alien — it was disruptive.

These days, women are more empowered to break free of society's expectations which are still there, just less universally accepted. The changes are noticeable not only in the workplace, but also in sports. In previously male-dominated sports like soccer or rugby, nowadays there is a fierce competition of female teams.

In the old days, a woman who didn't dream of dedicating her life to her husband and children was considered to have something wrong with her. She was delusional in thinking that she could be the professional equal of a man. She was thought to be cold-hearted and narcissistic for spurning the role of self-sacrificing helpmate and mother. Men, on the other hand, were expected to be fierce competitors at work and benevolent dictators in their homes.

No one of either gender was encouraged to be themselves. It is a blessing that young people today have difficulty even imagining the idea of being forced into a pre-defined role, without any consideration given to who they really are or what they would like to become.

While doing research for this book, I looked at comic-book superheroes (34,476 "comic-book" characters were analyzed)[12] and found some interesting statistics.

Nearly three-quarters (73.3%) of comic-book heroes are men. Only 26.7% of all DC and Marvel characters are female and barely more than one in ten (12%) of mainstream superhero comics have female protagonists. To make matters worse, female characters are often hyper-sexualized, unnecessarily brutalized, stereotyped, and used as tokens. They tend, also, to rely on stereotypically 'female' super-skills such as empathy, intellect, and telepathy, rather than physical power. The male characters, however, are often portrayed as having great physical strength, along with remarkable technological skills.

When female characters do have some extraordinary physical abilities, they are often tied to sex and emotions. The ability to create emotional and physical states, such as sleep, fear, and pleasure by means of pheromones, for example, occurs five times as often in a female character. Sonic scream appears in twice as many female characters as male. A hair-related superpower is something common for female characters, while being an extremely rare talent amongst men.

So yes, we are still educated that boys should be boys and girls should be girls. According to this view, boys should have a highly developed Gut Brain, something less favorable for women or girls. Women should have a huge Heart Brain full of compassion, and they should love, admire, and encourage Gut Brain behavior in their men, because that was what made them good providers and protectors.

Many of the old attitudes linger. There is still a lot of stereotyping going on in our education and in the business world. Most positions on executive boards are still held by men. And the competitive 'Me' attitude (Gut Brain) that is needed to compete in many business settings is still encouraged in boys, while often being discouraged in girls. To excel in the professional world, a certain amount of Gut Brain drive seems to be required.

The fact that the portrayal of masculinity as strong and femininity as caring is fully ingrained in our society is clear when we look at Hofstede's cultural dimensions theory. One dimension is named 'masculinity vs femininity'. 'Masculinity' describes a society's preference for achievement, heroism, assertiveness, and material rewards for success. The society at large is more competitive. On the contrary, the theory uses 'femininity' to demonstrate a society's preference for cooperation, modesty, caring for the weak, and quality of life. The society at large is more consensus-oriented.

If you are curious in how countries score, visit Hofstede's website at https://geerthofstede.com. A little teaser: For masculinity, Sweden has an index of 5, the Netherlands 14, Australia 61, the USA 62, the UK 66 and Japan 95.[13]

So just imagine how these scores will play out in the behavior of men in those countries and what that means if they become your partner?

When I was reading an article about Janine van den Berg[14] (the first female police chief on the board of Interpol), it struck me once again how we are conditioned to think we are different because of our gender.

In the interview, they asked her if a female police chief acts differently than a male one.

She replied, "You have to be really careful thinking like that, because before you know it you are generalizing, but as a rule men have more masculine traits, like decisiveness, and women have more feminine traits, like communication. I have both". Although she says not to generalize, she continues to label the traits as men- or women-specific.

What is the biggest problem with calling them 'feminine' and 'masculine' traits? Equal and happy, healthy relationships between men and women will stay on a Mission Impossible track.

Think about it. Why would you as a female adopt 'male' traits and run the risk of being called "masculine", or even worse, "bitchy", "bossy" or "working mom". Conversely, why would a man adopt 'female' traits with the risk of being called "feminine" or "pussy", "soft" or even "gay"?

By giving the traits the gender-neutral names of Heart Brain and Gut Brain — their original source — it becomes normal and acceptable for all of us to connect with them.

Because why would we not utilize all the resources we have inside us?

Why would a man not be willing to develop his Heart Brain if it brings him more 'success' at home and at work, and as collateral beauty makes him a better human being? Similarly, for women, why would they have an issue with saying that they have developed a more Gut Brain survival instinct, when it will benefit their relationships and career, not to mention boost their self-esteem?

Unfortunately, we do not have the chance to develop along this route from a young age, as our traditional education system does not support this way of thinking.

The myth and bad science of gender-linked inherent abilities

If you are one of the people who believe that, despite all this talk of equality, underneath it all there are some things that men have a greater aptitude for than women, and vice versa, let's look at the example of the Khasi and the Karbi. Neuroscience journalist, Maia Szalavitz, wrote about research done by Moshe Hoffman, who spent time with these two closely related groups in India, paying special attention to the women's roles.[15]

The Khasi and Karbi are very closely related. The groups only became separated a few hundred years ago, and marriages between them are quite common. Both groups are predominately farmers. They grow rice in a hilly region that gets abundant rainfall. Culturally, however, they are quite distinct.

The Karbi are living in a patrilineal way. The eldest son in each family inherits the property, which is owned by his father. Women are rarely allowed to own land. Political and religious leadership is male-dominated in the Karbi world and girls leave school, on average, nearly four years earlier than boys.

Among the Khasi, however, women are, without exception, the landowners. On the death of her mother, the youngest daughter inherits the land and property. It's frowned upon for men to even handle money. Cash earned by men working outside the family farm is usually given to their wives.

Both genders are equally educated, although men are the political and religious leaders.

Hoffman researched 1,279 people from four Khasi and four Karbi villages with a block puzzle that measured their spatial abilities — a marker of math and science aptitude.

The results were stunning.

Karbi men were 36% faster than Karbi women at solving the puzzles. About a third of the overall difference was attributable to the greater education received by the boys among the Karbi, and the rest seemed to be linked to other cultural differences.

Among the Khasi, however, it was an entirely different story.

In that society, in which boys and girls received similar education and men and women both played important roles, the difference in results between men and women was so small that it was not statistically significant.

Hoffman and his colleagues concluded that culture does matter. What made their study unique is that they could control the outcome for biological effects.

Hoffman's conversations with the people he was studying reinforced his observations. As an example, he spoke with an 18-year-old woman who had recently married and was living in the male-dominated Karbi tribe. He knew she had left school at the age of eight. He asked her, "Why didn't you keep going?" She replied, "That would be a complete waste of my time. Women are not smart enough to understand and I would never use it anyway."

Among the Khasi, however, it is men who are considered the weaker sex. Speaking to a Khasi woman, Hoffman confirmed that she handled the finances in her marriage. When asked why, she replied, "If you give a man money, he's just going to waste it on booze."

So, the whole idea that there are some groups or types of people who are better at some tasks or another, as a matter of science, is proven wrong.

We cannot blame our gender!

If it lies anywhere, the fault is that we permit ourselves and others to harbor such notions. When you do that, you end up with people believing they are less capable, and then, like the 18-year-old Karbi bride, they don't even try.

What can we do about it?

For starters, we can stop conditioning our children to behave in a solely Gut Brain way for boys and Heart Brain way for girls. Competition, winning or losing, all depends on the Gut Brain. Compassion, teamwork, and trust are the Heart Brain's domain. When we raise our children to believe that one is the strong suit of boys and the other of girls, we set them up for trouble both in their lives and their relationships.

There are no Feminine and Masculine traits. Only Head, Heart and Gut Brain traits.

Reason five: We underestimate the power that trauma, abuse or bullying have on our Three Brains

Based on our childhood and teen experiences, and painful or traumatic experiences in our lives, our Gut Brain, Heart Brain and Head Brain change in their understanding of the world and human relationships.

Every painful or traumatic experience that is connected to survival is encoded by the Gut Brain and when it is connected to relationships, by the Heart Brain. When we are seeking to understand both ourselves and others, we cannot ignore the fundamental experiences that have shaped our world views.

When somebody has experienced abuse or anything that made them afraid or feel unsafe, you can be certain their Heart Brain is scarred, and their Gut Brain is constantly on guard. The powerful feelings that those emotions and feelings elicit influence decisions that that person makes about life, love and risk taking, far more than any other intellectual process, even if the individual is not consciously aware of them.

I am 'lucky' to have had a personal experience to analyze myself. The very first seed of this book was planted in my Heart and Gut Brains when I was a little kid. When I was four years old, I spent 2 weeks quarantined in a hospital room. I had gone in for a simple procedure — my tonsils had to come out. But afterward I came down with a particularly nasty variety of the measles.

I had to be isolated from anyone I could infect — which was the whole human race. Imagine you're four years old and confined in a room, cut off from the world by glass and double doors. No visitors, not even my parents. The medical people who came into my room had to wear filters over their noses and mouths. I was being held in solitary confinement by a virus I could not see and did not understand.

It was then that I experienced how my Head Brain, Heart Brain and Gut Brain were working or not working, and how they stored memories — although it took me 45 years to truly grasp what the deeper parts of my brain were taking from this experience. At the time, all I knew was that part of me was happy to have my mum or dad visiting and felt heart broken to see them leave. Another part of me was afraid of the needles the nurses who where visiting might be bearing. Yet another part of my mind was just trying to make sense of it all but did not have the capacity to do this.

It took me years to understand that my different reactions were, in fact, my three different Brains, each experiencing in their own way what I was going through. My Gut Brain was afraid of the pain inflicted by my medical caregivers. My Heart Brain felt alone and abandoned. And my Head Brain was trying desperately to understand why all this was happening to me.

I turned five in that room. At my 'birthday party', the nurses came in to give me some cake, and my parents waved at me through the window.

So, what did my different Brains take away from this experience? My Gut Brain learned how to survive. My Heart Brain learned that the people you love might leave you behind, and that people can mislead you. My Heart Brain also learned to please in order to get affection so that people would be nice to me, so my Gut Brain had to learn to hide my true feelings from the doctors and nurses.

As a result, my Gut Brain learned not to trust. Eventually, it started controlling my Heart Brain, telling it not to trust the doctors and nurses.

If you look at this through an adult's eyes, the whole thing changes. When a grown-up goes to the hospital, their Head Brain knows why and understands what is going to happen. You know by then that when people say everything will be okay, it's not a promise, it's to boost your morale. The brain of a five-year-old, however, has neither the life experience nor the cognitive development to accept and understand what is happening. Hence, my hospital experience was a traumatic education for all of my Three Brains.

I developed a fear of rejection from women. I learned to not express my own needs, and to please women so that they would like me, and would neither hurt me nor leave me. When I received attention from them, it made my heart beat faster — not the best thing to do if you are trying to build a solid relationship with only one partner.

I did not know that my heart had a void (parents that were not allowed to be with me and nurses who could hurt me) that needed to be filled. It was only after years of learning from workshops, and experts in therapy and coaching, and adding to this knowledge my own ideas from helping clients and patients who were making the same mistakes as me, that I was gradually able to understand my own experiences and to re-educate my Three Brains to deal with the world in a different way.

Is it strange that I could not sustain a deep connection to another person? Looking back, absolutely not! I was a walking statistical validation of how difficult creating and sustaining true connections can be. 41% of first marriages end in divorce, 60% of second marriages end in divorce, 73% of third marriages end in divorce.[16]

> After each disaster, I became stronger but not smarter. What I learned came from deep reflection and it came in baby steps.

One of the reasons that I did not learn all the lessons when they were presented to me is because in my work life, these traits were beneficial. They made me run the extra mile in sales or when working with clients/ patients. I realize now all these behaviors and beliefs were not the real me, but the adapted me.

When I worked with people in teams or individually, I learned and observed that most of the issues about trust, communication, respect, and honesty were rooted in a disconnected Head, Heart or Gut Brain and a dominant communication from one of them. Most of the time, our Brains are misaligned — and that misalignment is rooted in our earliest experiences and our education/socialization. When we want to connect with other people, especially with a partner, we must free our Brains from all our positive and negative experiences/education and talk to them with one voice, a considered, integrated voice that is rooted in all three of our Brains, making sure that the connection we make is safe and sincere.

Trauma distorts our relationship compass

Trauma affects different parts of the Mind in different ways. The three parts of your Mind have very different priorities. Even the same experience will affect the Three Brains differently.

Your Gut Brain reacts to things that affect safety and survival. If something seems dangerous or frightening, your Gut Brain will never forget the feeling — even if no specific memory of what provoked it can be recalled. It will avoid similar situations at all cost. A Gut Brain trauma has all the force of an instinctual reaction. Some people call these 'triggers'.

Your Heart Brain is looking at things that affect relationships and connections to other people — lovers, families and the people you meet in day-to-day life.

But what happens when any of those Brains have bad experiences? How can those experiences influence — for good or ill — the decisions we make later in life? And how can we re-train our Brains to change, so that the lessons of a traumatic experience are not misapplied to situations that are not traumatic?

The answer, as I'm sure you can anticipate (thank you, Head Brains) is shaped by what each Brain has learned, how it was learned, and how the experience resonates with each Brain's focus and priorities.

A traumatized Gut Brain is like a bull in a China shop

What traumatizes the Gut? Everything that threatens our survival, especially when we cannot flee, fight, or resolve the problem immediately. The trauma experience and used coping mechanism stays stuck in our Gut as a warning signal and guideline on how to act in perceived similar situations; it connects with feelings/emotions such as fear, anger and rage. An example is a war veteran who, while walking in their home town with their partner, hears a loud, unexpected noise and ducks as though under fire.

Everything that triggers a Gut Brain reaction to safety threats, or to heartbreak at disconnection/betrayal, will be retained. Gut Brains don't forget what they have learned. The point of Gut Brain learning is to avoid such experiences in the future.

To understand Gut Brain trauma, we must look at it in several ways.

Firstly, Gut Brain learning is not intrinsically bad. Burning your hand on a hot stove is something that you should only experience once. The question is whether that experience creates a wound or scar that will shape — or be misapplied in — future decision-making. If the lesson learned is to stay away from all stoves, cooking, and kitchens, then the result of the trauma will be debilitating, and will set the learner up for a lifetime of unhealthy (and expensive) eating habits.

Secondly, your Gut Brain has the positive intention of keeping you safe and healthy, even if it doesn't always seem that way. If you had three extremely devastating breakups and the Gut Brain decided to turn your heart off so you can never fall in love again, we can certainly question how good this is for your health(!), but can't argue that it helped to save your heart from pain.

What is trauma and how does it affect our Gut Brain and our relationships?

The official definition of trauma is a terrifying event or ordeal that a person has experienced, witnessed, or learned about — especially one that is life threatening or that causes physical harm.

When it happens, the normal reaction is dissociation, a disconnect between the person experiencing the traumatic event and their sense of self. If you have not experienced it yourself (and I sincerely hope you have not), you have almost certainly heard someone who has been through a traumatic event saying that, "it seemed to be happening to someone else and I was just watching it happen." There is no better description of traumatic dissociation than that.

This feeling of disconnection can persist and become what we call 'Post Traumatic Stress Disorder' (PTSD). In my opinion, it would be better to call it 'Post Traumatic Trauma Disorder'. It can create a wall between a person's sense of themselves and their own mind, body, and community. In the short-term, however, it is a great survival strategy. In that horrible moment, the Gut Brain or Heart Brain anesthetizes you from the pain and fear.

The problem in the long term, however, is that the Gut Brain will never forget what happened — and the Heart Brain is unlikely to — and the effects of that traumatic event will shape that person's reactions in the future — often to events or people who had nothing to do with, or any knowledge of, the traumatic event.

When we talk about trauma, it's important to look at how deep and intense the scar is and the type of trauma itself.

A single trauma is bad enough, but when a traumatic experience continues over time, it can be truly devastating, for example, a horrendous breakup or child abuse. The age when it happens makes a dramatic difference. When you are young, any trauma is immediately installed in the Gut and Heart Brains.

AN UNRESOLVED TRAUMA, NIGHT TERRORS

I once saw a client who experienced a break-in during the night. She was tied up and left there for a couple of hours until the neighbors, noticing that her front door was open, went in and found her. It happened when she was in her 20s. When she came to see me, years later, she still had problems falling asleep, and would have discussions with her (ex-)partners about locking the door and checking if everything was secure before going to bed. Every little sound in the night startled her awake in a panic. This even led to a breakup with one partner, who could not deal with this. Her Gut Brain could not distinguish between the normal sounds of a neighborhood at night, associating them all with her previous terrifying experience. Over time, we worked on bringing her Head Brain into the mix — and it learned how to soothe the panicky Gut Brain.

There are, of course, many types of traumatic experiences. In addition, what is traumatic for one person might not be for another, or it might be traumatic in a different way. In addition, of course, each Brain will understand a traumatic event differently. Rather than exhaust ourselves with the details, let's focus on the lesson to be learned about traumas of all kinds.

Any experience that a person has, especially when they are young, will shape their view of the world. It forms their views of what can happen, what should happen and whether they can trust parents, partners, or friends.

Traumas also, quite often, result in a person creating a set of reflexes — nearly instinctual reactions designed to avoid something like that happening again, or to protect the person from further damage if it does.

> I doubt there: "is a person alive whose decision-making is not influenced by some traumatic event?"

Such experiences are often at the root of bad or inappropriate decisions that we make in our lives and relationships. Traumas provoke unthinking reactions. There are few times in life when such reactive decisions are the same ones you would have made if you had a chance to think it over.

The intention of this book is not to be a therapy book and solve all our traumas, but much more to recognize them, and become aware of how they influence us, our partners, and our relationships. In the coming chapters, we will dive into how our Three Brains work and communicate, and how allowing our Heart and Head Brains into the discussion can help the Gut Brain get over its 'gut reaction'.

Abuse: The most damaging trauma of all for our relationships

When someone is mentally, physically, or sexually abused, their Three Brains can interpret what happened in extremely different ways, which in turn influences what the person does in later life to protect themselves from further injury. We have come to understand in recent years that such experiences are shockingly common.[17]

Based on official statistics, more than one in four women (27%) and one in six men (16%) in the United States were sexually abused as children (source: National Victim Center and the Crime Victims Research & Treatment Center). Current estimates on the rate of child sexual abuse range from one to ten children per 100 children under the age of 18. In addition, seven countries reported that more than one-fifth of the girls there had been abused (37.8% in Australia, 32.2% in Costa Rica, 31% in Tanzania, 30.7% in Israel, 28.1% in Sweden, 25.3% in the US, and 24.2% in Switzerland.[18]

A child who was abused is invariably traumatized and, 90% of the time, that trauma will continue to affect them in their adult lives. Besides that, their sense of trust has been broken, and they have learned strange ways about how 'love' should be given or received. People who have experienced this, as seen in my therapy room, all have issues to varying degrees with trust, commitment, and intimacy.

What do these experiences do to a person? And how do they influence their ability to make decisions later in life?

HOW A MESSED UP PARENT DESTROYS THE HAPPINESS FOR HIS SON

I had a male client whose father used aggression and terror as a parenting tool. "You have to keep the children afraid so that they will listen to you," was his idea of responsible fatherhood. As long as he could remember, my client told me, he hid in his room instead of going out to play. (Keeping yourself safe is a Gut Brain response.)

His brother committed suicide at 40. His sister, who had grown up being told she was ugly, had turned her body into a playground for plastic surgeons. So, my client was doing better than his siblings. Even so, he suffered from severe anxiety (his Gut Brain was on constant alert) and commitment issues (his Heart Brain could not trust). If he thought somebody disliked him, he would do anything to earn their approval. (Heart Brain and Gut Brain working together to reduce the risk of rejection.)

If you met this client in everyday life, he would strike you as happy, stable, well-educated, well-groomed, and polite. He was articulate and friendly. On the outside, he was a well-adjusted 50-something, with no more than the normal bumps and bruises. By all appearances, he was a catch.

If you spent some time with him, though, you would become aware that he always started a sentence with, "Don't get me wrong..." or, "I don't mean to say..." He peppered every conversation with clarifications and preemptive apologies, such as, "My intention is..."

From our three-Brain perspective, we can dissect what was going on — and it was sad. His Heart Brain wanted to and was trying to connect. His Gut Brain wanted to make a connection too, by making itself accommodating and inoffensive. But every time connection seemed possible, the Gut Brain took control for a moment to cushion itself from the possibility of being rejected again.

The closer you got to this guy, the more frightened he would become. In the end, his Gut Brain would shut down the Heart Brain's desire to connect. The risk of being vulnerable and getting hurt was more than it could tolerate. The result? A lifetime of failed connections. He had never had a long-lasting relationship because he could not trust in committing to or opening up to any potential partner.

You are sure to know — and may have been burned by — someone like this.

Example: Using weight as protection after being sexually abused

A couple of years ago, I saw a female client in her 50s, who came back to work on her weight after I had helped her to successfully stop smoking two years earlier.

She said that it was time to work on her weight. She was 110kg.

When I asked her how she had arrived at this decision, she replied emotionally, "Six months ago, my sister got married. During the year before the marriage, I lost 40kg so that I would look great at her wedding, and I did. However, I was in a constant state of panic. I even had a panic attack at the wedding when a nice guy said that he thought I was really beautiful and asked for my number."

"After the wedding, I gained 40kg within two months, by eating all the ice cream I could buy, and really stuffed myself like a goose."

The reason for her behavior was that when she was between the ages of 8 and 12, she was sexually abused by a family member. As she was from an Italian family, she had never told anyone, even up to that moment, because it could have ruined the family relationship.

The abuse stopped when she was 12 years old because she started to eat a lot and gain weight. She used her weight as a protection mechanism from being sexually abused, as the Gut Brain thought, "Let's make ourselves less attractive for the predator." Forty years later, she still had the same mechanism, and it had ruined some of her relationships because her (ex-)partners could not deal with it. Thankfully, her current husband knew how to avoid the land mines.

Every compliment she received on her looks caused her anxiety. She had developed a mechanism of not wanting to be perceived as attractive. Her Gut Brain learned this protection mechanism when she was 12 and overruled all the other possible life experiences for the next 40 years.

The poison of a traumatized Heart — betrayal, grief, and bullying

We are social animals. Our Heart Brain is driven by a desire to connect, and when it finds someone to bond with, the two Heart Brains literally establish a heart-to-heart connection. The energy of our heart can be detected nine meters outside our body, and when people are really connecting with each other, they can create a heart coherence in which their two hearts beat at the same intensity and pace. Did you think that Bruce Springsteen's song Two Hearts was a pop tune? It is, in fact, a well-researched discourse on a medical phenomenon...

Betrayal

Maybe you know the feeling of 'being loved' — the feeling that someone else is loving you. It is like your heart is swelled by the energy coming from somebody else. But, if that is taken away, our hearts feel broken. When we don't feel loved and cared for, our heart feels empty. The expression "finding my other half" can feel as if it is literally true.

In fact, Plato, the ancient Greek philosopher, in his Symposium, relates a tale that the gods had, at the dawn of time, split human beings in half, and that they were fated to search until they found their missing soulmate who would complete them.

It is ten times worse when betrayal is involved in the breakup, because it cuts our trusting Heart in two. We start doubting our Heart instinct so the Gut Brain has to step in to rescue us. In many cases, the Heart Brain will be shut down by the Gut Brain to prevent our Heart from falling in love again or trusting someone else.

EXAMPLE: HOW TO HAVE A RELATIONSHIPS IF YOU ARE UNABLE TO TRUST?

I still remember the client who visited me because she felt she could not trust anyone. She was a successful, emotionally intelligent lady in her early 40s. She was single and wanted very much to be in a loving relationship but had never been able to sustain one. She told me that the men she had been involved with had a common complaint: She did not share her feelings or emotions. One of her ex-boyfriends had called her a "closed oyster".

She thought that her problem with trusting people was rooted in a traumatic betrayal she had experienced when she was a teenager. Her best friend in high school was someone she felt very close to. She told all her secrets to this girl. As time passed, however, the friend came to resent that others considered her to be attractive and smart. She grew jealous and critical and began to spread rumors and nasty stories. Ultimately, the friend seduced her boyfriend and ruined her reputation in the school.

After that experience, she, or rather, her Heart Brain, was less open to people and did not trust that her potential partners or her girlfriends would not betray her. The wound her Heart Brain had received in high school had tainted every relationship she had ever had. Whenever her Heart Brain felt love or a real connection, her Gut Brain would step in to say, "Don't go there! Remember what happened to us in high school!"

Grief

Grief can be the hardest or the easiest issue to solve, depending on the situation. For example, when you have a painful breakup, then later find the real love of your life, the grief is extremely easily resolved. On the other hand, when grief is for somebody who died, it is harder to resolve. The most common reason for this is that our Head Brain reminds our Heart Brain of the good times with that person.

It is easy to see that manipulation and betrayal are traumatic for the Heart Brain, as our hearts are predisposed to love and trust. When love is denied and trust is broken at the same time, it can cause deep and lasting scars. When this happens, the Gut Brain and Head Brain also respond. The Gut Brain focuses on safety, and will build walls to ensure that such a trauma is never permitted to happen again. The Head Brain will keep us awake at night, trying to answer the questions, "Why and how could this have happened to me? What did I miss?"

Because betrayal and manipulation are things that we become aware of after the damage is done, our Heart Brain can come to distrust the Head and Gut Brains for not figuring out what was going on, and not protecting the trusting and vulnerable Heart. As a result, although we would love to make a new connection, we do not trust enough to connect with someone else.

Researcher, Bessel van der Kolk (Professor, Harvard University and Professor of Psychiatry, Boston University School of Medicine), concluded that, however wounded, our need for Heart Brain connections never diminishes.[19] Very few of us can tolerate being separated from others for any length of time. We will do almost anything (from playing a victim, blaming, fighting to self harm) to get the human connection we crave. This is the reason that extended periods of solitary confinement is, by itself, considered to be a form of torture by both the Geneva Convention and the United Nations.

Physical or social isolation is so painful — especially to a child — that it is often the root of destructive behavior. If attempts to gain approval or positive attention of the family or group fail, then the Gut Brain takes over and tries other ways of getting attention. Even negative attention is better than being ignored. Many of the people in our lives who seem to thrive on conflict, who act defiantly, who file lawsuits, get into bar fights, or take extraordinary risks, are lonely and willing to do anything to get others to notice them.

EXAMPLE: THE PAIN OF REJECTION AND BETRAYAL

The kind of breakup that leaves the worst scar is when someone is replaced for another, with betrayal on top.

A good-looking guy in his 40s came into my office one day. He had already told me on the phone that he had trust issues and a broken heart.

Without me even asking, his story came gushing out.

He had had an amazing relationship with a woman for a some years, but she had broken off the relationship a little less than six months earlier. He said that it had been great on all levels: there had been intellectual connection, they had shared the same life values, the sex had been fantastic and they had felt extremely compatible.

I hear you thinking, "Why the breakup, why did she leave him?"

As they both worked internationally, they sometimes did not see each other for a couple of weeks but had contact every day on FaceTime, or on Messenger.

Just before he was coming back from his last trip abroad, he had a nauseating feeling that they had become disconnected.

In a text he asked her, "What's happening? I have a strange feeling we're disconnected." (Signs that he had developed an energetic Heart Brain connection).

Then she dropped the bomb. She had been seeing somebody for the last three weeks. And she wanted to pursue that relationship.

He said that he was in total shock because he had not seen any signs at all. In the texts they exchanged after this devastating message, she also shared that my client was the person she had always dreamed of as a partner.

I thought, "What is wrong with her, what need was not met that made her do something so 'strange'?"

It turned out that she had met a man who was 25 years older than her. Why was she attracted to him? When she was 12 years old, her dad died. He had been her hero and the center of her world. She had also had two good friends, also much older than her, both 'replacements' for her dad, and both had died many years ago.

She had a traumatized heart as result of her dad's death, and her Heart Brain wanted to fill up that void with a surrogate father.

My client said, "My biggest issue is that it makes me feel that, although I'm her perfect guy, I am not good enough. I am not worthy of love. I do not trust my own heart or judgments any more when I meet a woman. Somewhere I have a voice/feeling inside me that says, "They can say they love you. They can act as if they love you. But, in the end, they will take their love away and abandon you."

So, in this case, we can see how a broken heart that is not healed can cause a lot of relationship issues in the future. She wanted to heal her broken heart with a relationship based on her past issues, instead of going for a relationship based on the future.

He essentially experienced insecure attachment. He gave away his heart to somebody else, trusting her to take care of it/him, and believing that she was doing the same. Without a 'reason' to give his Heart Brain, the love/trust was taken away (panic: "I am left alone."), the Head Brain had issues with grasping this concept and could not help him out, the Gut Brain was working overtime to save the Heart Brain from excruciating pain. Being left alone is a fundamentally scary thing for babies; it is ingrained in our hardwiring. As a result, his Gut and Head Brains decided not to trust women anymore. When I observed him, his immobilization (Gut Brain) was turned on to protect him from pain. His fight or flight response was frustrated, not to know who or what to attack or defend him from.

Bullying and the devastating scars they can leave behind

We all know bullies. Some of us have been their victims. Other times we might be shocked to learn that the tactics we used to get our way or win a point meet the definition of bullying behavior. In its simplest form, bullying is the tactic of trying to exploit someone else's physical or psychological weakness to gain power over them.

Although much of the current focus on bullying is on school settings and young people, it is by no means confined to school yards or young people. It is nonetheless a common issue at school. Almost one out of every four students (22%) reports that they have been bullied during their school years. Bullying has a profound effect on how far we dare to trust people, how we interact with people, and how much openness and affection we dare to show.[20]

There are dozens of books on the subject, and hundreds of organizations that aim to combat bullying. Bullies have been a problem as long as there have been social groups. The birth of the internet has made the problem especially pernicious, as they have come to infect every level of social contact and discourse. Looking at the issue through the lens of the Three Brains Theory, however, can help us cope better with the bullies that we will inevitably come across in our lives.

What is a bully? Bullies are people who try to gain power over others. This behavior is usually based on their own pain of being disconnected earlier in their life. Bullying is carried out by a misaligned Gut Brain and a Heart Brain that is turned off. (More about this in Chapter 11: 'Children also have Three Brains (only two are booted up)')

Dominant Heart Brain people are vulnerable to bullying because they have an overwhelming desire to be liked and accepted. They are lovers, not fighters. A bully can exploit that by holding out the carrot of being included in their group, in order to "bend" their target to their will.

The traumatized Head Brain — when logic fails, what is left?

Dominant Head Brain people are pitifully also vulnerable to bullies in a different way. A Head Brain's goal, of course, is always to figure out how things work. They are less interested in physical appearances, that's the Gut Brain's domain. Bullies have a preference to use the Head Brain people for their own benefit at school or work, to use the talent of the Head Brain person and present it as if it was theirs. They will physically threaten the Head Brain person to follow their orders if they do not want to be hurt; no right-thinking Head Brain is going to contradict that. Any Head Brain person with a lick of sense however, is also going to be constantly re-assessing to find the bully's own weakness and come up with a plan to turn the tables on him or her as soon as the chance arises.

According to researcher Ivan Yakovlev, our Head Brain is a servant of our other two Brains.[21] You might think, therefore, that it cannot be traumatized by itself. Even so, experiences have a profound effect on both the thoughts that we have and the way we formulate them. With all the discussions we have had about the Head Brain being the home of logic and analysis, you might also expect that logic and an innate 'Scientific Method' are part of our Head Brain's standard equipment.

In one sense, they are. Our Head Brains try their best to understand the world around us by remembering experiences, observing other people, and making predictions based on that. So, in that sense, logical processes are at work.

But something as powerful and complicated as our Head Brain also needs to be able to filter good information from bad, relevant experiences and learning from things that are dissimilar or irrelevant. That level of insight requires a process of education. And the world is filled with people who want to train your brain to see the world as they do, or as they want you to. So, education requires critical thinking. The ability to think critically is not something we are born with; it is a discipline that needs to be developed. In short, Head Brains can become unmoored from the real world and start supplying us with misguided notions that it cannot distinguish from reality. When they do, we start making bad decisions based on errors in how we have interpreted our own lives and experiences.

Somewhere in our Head Brains, we all have lodged some irrational beliefs. They are not always a bad thing. For many people, accepting a belief on faith alone — like a religious philosophy — is an essential.

But there are many ways that a cognitive process can go awry and disrupt our ability to make good decisions.

In psychology, we call this 'cognitive distortion'. You can recognize this when people make generalizations such as, "It is always like this", or,

"This can never happen". It is also seen in 'black-and-white thinking', for example, "You are good" or, "You are bad"; there are no shades of grey.

Other instances of cognitive distortion are excessive rumination and over-analysis, usually when the person is in bed and would like to sleep instead.

You can also recognize it when people are using language of necessity, saying words like, 'should', 'must', or 'have to'.

Finally, people with cognitive distortion tend to jump to conclusions/mind reading/fortune telling and say things like, "Because of this, it is that", or, "I know what you think".

When people's Head Brains, due to an upsetting experience or incorrect information, start supplying these cognitive distortions, certain beliefs can be installed to make life 'easier'. These, in turn, can undermine the person's abilities to function and can cause real problems.

There are all sorts of coping mechanisms used by the Head Brain to deal with a trauma that it cannot explain. For example, beliefs like the ones listed below can prevent a person from making good, well-considered decisions:

- I am not good enough.
- Men/women cannot be trusted.
- I'm no good at…
- I'm fated to be…
- You can't get ahead if you are a woman.
- Relationships are just too hard.
- People will always let you down.
- I'll never be able to do what I want because…

Limiting beliefs like these are an indicator that some trauma is clouding the Head Brain's thinking. They are shortcuts, learned along the way, that skew a person's perception of reality.

Furthermore, our Head Brain is heavily influenced by visualization. Research shows that visualization — which uses imagination and memory — activates the same neurons that are engaged when we have the actual experience. This means that visualizing negative experiences or memories triggers all the negative emotional reactions that we had with the original experience, wiring them more deeply into our Brains.

As we now know from brain science research, "neurons that fire together wire together".[22] In other words, the more we train a memory, the stronger it becomes, and the more it will dominate our life. So, if we start constraining what we do because of limiting beliefs, those beliefs become stronger and stronger. We end up being unhappy in ourselves and impaired in our ability to relate to others.

EXPERIMENTAL PROOF: NEURONS THAT FIRE TOGETHER WIRE TOGETHER

A team of researchers from UCLA, USA, and the Weizmann Institute, Israel, showed TV programs, including Seinfeld and The Simpsons, to epileptic patients undergoing brain surgery, who had microelectrodes implanted in their Brains.

The researchers showed patients a series of five- to ten-second clips and made recordings from 100 neurons (nerve cells in the brain) that fired as they watched. They then distracted the patients. After some time, they asked the patients, "What comes to mind when you remember the Simpsons clip?"

The same neurons that fired when they watched that clip then fired when they remembered it. The same thing happened with the

Seinfeld clips — the neurons specific to the Seinfeld clips fired. In other words, the same neurons fire when a person experiences an event and subsequently remembers it.[23]

Mental illness makes lovers into both therapists and clients

There is another type of injury that can affect people's ability to connect to their Brains — or which prevents those Brains from functioning as they should. Sometimes this is caused by external experiences. More often, however, those experiences can exacerbate or reinforce a problem that was already there.

Culturally, in the Western world, we are not yet at a point at which people who have a mental illness or dysfunction are not stigmatized. Hopefully we will get there soon. Mental illnesses are incredibly common, and many are easily treated. Stigmatizing them only makes things worse for the people who deal with them and for society at large.

A research study that followed a generation estimated that about 80% of all people in the USA will experience a mental health issue of some kind in their lifetime.[24] The researchers believe that percentage holds true for people in most Western countries.

Mental health issues are real, they can be debilitating, and people are often too embarrassed to seek the help that could make them better. In the USA alone, one out of four people is currently living with major depression or anxiety.[25]

To a therapist like me, it is shocking that two-thirds of people with a known mental disorder never get professional help.[26] Stigma, discrimination, and neglect prevent people from seeking the care and treatment that could help them lead happier and more fulfilled lives. Where there is neglect, there is little to no understanding. Likewise, where there is no understanding, there is neglect.

Whether or not the troubles in your own life reach the level of clinical diagnosis, it is virtually certain that someone close to you is trying to cope with a significant mental issue. So how do we apply what we know about three-Brain communication to our interactions with people whose Brains are in turmoil?

Mental illnesses often involve a Brain other than the Head Brain. Anxiety is based on fear, so originates from the Gut Brain, while depression is initiated by the Heart.

It is becoming increasingly common that one partner in a relationship experiences poor mental health, causing the other to act as a kind of therapist. Most people are not educated in this role, which makes these relationships hard work.

As an example, a couple once visited me for advice. He was diagnosed with PTSD and depression, was on medication and on sick leave. The woman wanted advice on how to deal with him.

She loved him dearly, but was having issues dealing with him, as he was not the "happy enthusiastic guy he used to be". She dealt with the situation by taking more time for herself, spending more time at work and practicing sport every day. She had even recently signed up to run a marathon.

Although she was happy with her strategy, he felt as if she was avoiding him. She said that she didn't know how to deal with him for an entire evening. In the old days, they got along easily, but the evenings had become more serious, something she was struggling with. She felt that she had to be extra careful in her behavior and communication, which required an enormous amount of energy. She added that she did not want to be a therapist at home but was being made to feel that way.

After reading all of this, you could wonder is there still hope?

The answer: Yes we can have amazing relationships!

Although we all come into the world predisposed to be happy and healthy in our Head, Heart and Gut Brains, a good number of us will get messed up based on an insecure attachment with one or both of our parents[27] (see more in Chapter 11's section called 'The first two years').

This is not to say that parents set out to mess with our Brains and propel us onto psychiatrists' couches. Parents are only human, too. They have their own issues and traumas to deal with. They make mistakes. No matter how good their intentions however, things rarely turn out according to plan. If they did, we wouldn't have to spend so much of our energy building and fueling our Head Brain. It is important to acknowledge that almost every parent does whatever he or she can to make life easy and comfortable for their children.

In the case of my client, his father told him much later in life that he thought he was doing the right thing. He had been bruised by the realities of a hard life and was trying to prepare his children for an unkind world. It wasn't until his son killed himself that the father had to confront the damage he had done.

So, gaining insight on how the Head, Heart and Gut Brains operate is no parlor game. It can be a matter of life or death.

Is there something here for us to work with? Absolutely. We can all learn what drives our own Brains' decisions, then use those same techniques to recognize and communicate with our partners, friends, colleagues, managers, and everyone else in our lives.

You can educate, adjust, and align your Three Brains, and you can help others do the same. No matter who you are, or how old you are, your Brains are capable of learning and changing. They are not made of stone.

Conclusion: We all can have happy and healthy relationships! And yes, it takes work 😊.

Section 2:

WHAT IS YOUR
DOMINANT BRAIN?

3.

Who is your boss? Your Head, Your Heart or Your Gut?

The only reason we have Brains at all is that we need them to make decisions. Even if you're a Komodo dragon and that basic Gut Brain is all you have, it's there to enable you to choose between options. "Eat it, attack it, or hide?" might be the biggest decision a dragon ever faces. But if its Gut Brain couldn't do its job of choosing the safest option, there would never have been more than one generation of Komodo dragons. Their Komodo Gut Brains however, have kept them with us. Human Brains, of course, are infinitely more complex. Reptiles don't have to balance the decisions made by a second or third Brain.

By understanding how our Three Brains are making decisions based on our visceral reactions (Gut Brain), our emotions (Heart Brain), and our thoughts (Head Brain), we will be able to understand ourselves and communicate better. As a bonus, we can understand other people better and create a happy, healthy relationship with them.

When you think about it, we need to make decisions about everything. Even breathing can involve decision-making from our Brains. Yes, basic respiration is an autonomic nervous system process but your Brains can influence your breathing by deciding to speed it up or slow it down. Something as simple as holding your breath underwater requires a decision by your Head Brain to tell the autonomic system to postpone inhalation until it's safe to do so.

You can also easily observe this when you increase your walking pace or run up or down the stairs. We can also regulate our breathing through mind control and in some forms of yoga.

Your Brains are constantly talking to one another — updating their cerebral teammates about their internal processes, external sensations, feelings, emotions, and thoughts. When the Gut Brain feels safe and satisfied, it can relax and allow the Heart and Head Brains to do what they are supposed to do — connect, learn, and think.

So, in 'normal' (non-threatening) daily life, when we are not feeling that our lives or safety are in peril, we can interact with other people, feel love, think about work, and get on with life.

'Mindfulness' is a word some use to describe the technique they use to align their Three Brains. In that 'mindful' state, the Gut Brain is at ease. So, when we talk about who is the boss, it changes depending on what action or decision is being weighed up. If we are alert to some danger, it will always be the Gut Brain that takes control. The Gut Brain is a watchdog. Even when it seems to be napping, it's always aware of what's going on and is ready, in a heartbeat, to bite a burglar (or the mail carrier). Or, depending on how vulnerable you feel, it could be more like a rabbit — always twitching its ears for the sound of a predator.

Rule of thumb

When our Gut Brain is confident enough it shows trust, like the lion that walks in the savanna's. When our Gut Brain is more hesitant it will likely follow a more submissive or path of least resistance, like Scar in the Lion King.

When our Heart Brain is confident it acts from empathy and compassion. When our Heart is hurt it will express neediness and pleasing behavior.

Last but not least when our Head Brain is doing fine we are full of curiosity but when it is blocked it is full of judgements.

When there are no burglars or foxes about, the Gut Brain retreats into the background. If we are safe, and in a family or relationship setting, it's usually the Heart Brain that is running the show. If there is some complexity to be sorted out, the Head Brain will take over for a while.

When the Gut Brain feels or thinks it should take over (whether for a valid reason or a false alarm), it immediately pulls the circuit breakers on the Heart Brain and the Head Brain. "There is no time to ponder options. Right now, I'm looking out for me and only me." Gender makes no difference. The instant we feel unsafe, the Gut Brain takes over. Communication and actions will be focused on self-preservation and nothing else.

4.

Do the free Three Brains Preference Assessment to have your insight in how your Brains decide

Knowing yourself is the first step in mastering any relationship, so doing the Brains Preference assessment provides you a quick, free and simple inside in which Brain in you is the most dominant.

WHEN YOU VISIT THE WEBSITE

www.3brainsacademy.com/3-Brains-preference-assesment

you can do the free Three Brains Preference Assessment and that provides you a beautiful insight in how you make your unconscious default decisions and communicate.

5.

Our Three Brains' strengths and weaknesses

Our Three Brains make decisions in different ways

This is an important concept to remember when you are seeking a soulmate or even just having a conversation with someone.

The Head Brain's thoughtful consideration does not happen when the Heart or Gut Brains have been activated. Similarly, the Heart Brain's capacity for connection and compassion are offline when we are in Gut Brain-driven survival mode. You could see this as a pyramid. Only when the lower Brain is content can we can go up to a more sophisticated level of thinking.

The Gut Brain's strength — the watchdog, 'Me' first

The **Gut Brain:** All the actions are based on our lust for life and therefore includes all the survival instincts with sensations like fear, desire, disgust, and rage. When the Gut Brain is making decisions, our communication and behavior is based on those sensations of desire, fear, anger and lust, and is always focused on 'Me'. As a result when this brain is in charge and only it is in charge, it will show controlling and power driving behavior, with the sole intention of self protection.

The highest needs of our Gut Brain are achieving personal success, establishing safety, getting food and reproduction. It lives by the mantra: how can I make the best of life?

When our ancestors climbed out of their aquatic primordial homes, it was their Gut Brain that was propelling them. Dry land felt like a safer neighborhood to raise their children than a sea teeming with predators. From that time to this, Gut Brains have never lost sight of their priorities as watchdog, namely to keep their owner safe and to meet physical needs. That first Brain, primitive as it may seem, is the root of our evolutionary success — and that of every other animal on the planet. We were able to survive.

Before we start looking at the relatively sophisticated thinking of the other Brains that are crowded into our Homo sapiens head, let's take a moment to appreciate how remarkably successful Gut Brains have been. Every animal on Earth is the result of millions of years of Gut Brain success in keeping them alive and healthy long enough to reproduce. But, whether it's in your own head or that of a codfish, the Gut Brain does not think or act consciously. Its reactions are a blend of instinctive and learned responses. Gut Brains want to escape fear, pain, and hunger. They seek safety and the satisfaction of physical desires. Because of that, Gut Brains are amazingly powerful, decisive, and creative in their own way. When you (or any other person or creature) feel endangered, the Gut Brain takes the reins. Gut Brains don't think in shades of grey. To them, survival is a black-and-white concept.

Our Gut Brain decides whether or not we want to react to something or someone — be it to fight, flee, surrender, eat or mate with. It controls our 'gut reaction' to whether a situation or person is safe or a threat.

The simple notion of agreeing or disagreeing with something is a Gut Brain task. In small non-emergency decisions, our Gut Brains consult the Head Brain to weigh in with its judgment. Before it does, the Gut Brain has made its own decision — which it compares to what the Head Brain advises. If it thinks the Head Brain is advocating something foolhardy, it will protest and try to put a stop to it.

You know that queasy feeling you get when you've made a decision that part of you thinks is not right? What you are feeling is your Gut Brain saying, "I do not like this!" Gut Brains work with feelings and emotions, not words. Making you feel just a little nauseated — just a taste of fear — can be remarkably effective. In fact, fear is the Gut Brain's ultimate weapon. Also in its arsenal of feelings are anger, rage, disgust, and craving.

The Gut Brain's weakness — a blunt instrument

The Gut Brain is a blunt instrument. Its decisions are not foolproof, in part because it has no store of facts or logic against which to determine if a fear is real, or whether a craving is to be suppressed or acted upon. Avoiding danger is such a high priority that Gut Brains are designed to act first and never ask questions. That makes it perfect for what it does. It keeps us alive and meets our physical needs. If you are an iguana, a chicken, or a carp, that Gut Brain is all you need. For the rest of us, it lacks some of the refinements we need to build families, grow crops, and do the other things that we need to survive in the modern world. It is not designed to think or feel for others.

Gut Brains learn powerful, but simple, lessons about the things that concern it: safety, avoiding pain, and gratifying physical needs and desires. Anything it learns stays learned and it applies that learned reaction in any situation that seems similar — whether it actually is similar. As you might imagine, teaching the Gut Brain to react differently is an extremely challenging task. It can be done. But words alone are not enough.

The Heart Brain's strengths — loving, caring and courageous

The Heart Brain: Every beat it makes is driven by the need for relationships and connection, it has a desire to bond. The sensations we become aware of include love, guilt, happiness, hope, joy, shame, sorrow, hate, and sadness. Because they are all based on connecting and belonging and are all about 'Us', they are essential in our relationships. It also means this Brain can only play a part in our decision-making when we feel safe enough to let our guard down and put the Gut Brain at rest, so that we can feel and nurture attachments.

> *The highest need of our Heart Brain is to belong by creating and feeling connections with others. It follows the Mantra: how can I help you?*

The Heart Brain evolved because the Gut Brain did not have the skills for family life. Animals with nothing but a Gut Brain often eat their young — something frowned upon in a community or a pack. An anatomist would place the Heart Brain's primary location in the **limbic brain**. (It may not be exclusive to mammals — but every animal on earth that consciously cares for its young is guided by a Heart Brain that shapes (but does not control) its decision-making.

The Heart Brain's domain is our emotional world — love, parental bonding and every variety of affection and interpersonal connection. It is our Heart Brain that compels us to seek out someone to bond with. It is where the emotional tools are stored that enable us to form families and communities.

One way to understand the function of the Heart Brain is to continue the canine analogy we made earlier. Just as the Gut Brain serves as a kind of watchdog — always on the alert for danger — the Heart Brain is your inner puppy — loving, uncritical, desperate to connect with and share affection with those around it.

The Heart Brain can shape and limit the Gut Brain's instinctual reactions. It tries (and often succeeds) to shift the Gut Brain's priorities to include other things that are crucial for health, life, and security, beyond those of animal survival. When a parent sacrifices comfort and safety to assist their child, a family member, or even a stranger, that is because the Heart Brain persuaded the Gut Brain to modify its instinctive selfish reaction. To go along with the Heart Brain's inclinations however, the Gut Brain must feel that it's safe.

Later, we will look more deeply into how your Heart Brain can persuade your Gut Brain to do what it wants — and even to modify its definition of 'self' to include others.

The Heart Brain's weaknesses — naïve, trusting and self-sacrificing

Heart Brains are optimistic, believe in the good of other people and are therefore often perceived as naïve. Heart Brains feel therefore they treasure emotional connections. Heart Brains believe in sharing and fairness. They believe the world is just, and that the love and care you give to others will always be reciprocated. If you only ever listened to your Heart Brain, you would go through the world with a childlike innocence, always trusting that other people are as open, honest, and as trusting as you are. As you can imagine, Heart Brains are open to manipulation and exploitation. Adolf Hitler's dog Blondi, had no doubt that he was the greatest guy in the world. Only a healthy and vigilant Gut Brain can keep a Heart Brain from getting into real trouble. It didn't end well for Blondi who, on Hitler's order, was fed a cyanide capsule to see if it would work.

On the other hand, wounded Heart Brains become outraged, all the more so because they never see the hurt coming. Discovering that it has been manipulated or betrayed is humiliating for the Heart Brain. And humiliation provokes hate and activates Gut Brain rage. A wounded, enraged Heart Brain could seek to hurt in return, because only then will its need for justice be satisfied. A well-tended Heart Brain is a joy to all around it. But a misdirected one can be a fetid swamp of clannishness, racism, and hostility.

Just as a generous Heart Brain can persuade the Gut Brain to include others into its sense of 'self', a wounded Heart Brain can infect the Gut Brain with malice and vindictiveness.

The Head Brain's strength — logic, knowledge and creativity

The Head Brain: This amazing Brain is solely focused on making logical analyses and decisions for the future, based on acquired (past) knowledge. It deals with intellectual sensations like anticipation, interest, surprise and wonder. All those things can influence our decisions. We can really use this Brain only when we are feeling safe enough or it is consulted by the Gut or Heart Brains. It cannot override the Gut Brain in situations that provoke fear. And, as we mentioned above, it has an almost impossible task trying to convince a Heart Brain to override an emotional decision.

The Highest need of our Head Brain is providing the correct predictions and 24/7 it is following its mantra: how does this work, what does it mean and what is the best way to do it?

Your Head Brain is what makes you, as a Homo sapien, different from all other creatures. It is the most recently evolved of the Three Brains (around two million years ago). A few of our higher-ape cousins also have a Head Brain, but it is more advanced in humans. Anatomists call it the **neocortex** — and it contains the structures that process language, abstract ideas and the awareness of time. As the newcomer, it is constantly chattering about what it sees — the future, re-evaluations of the past, the logic of our life and surroundings — while persuading the other Brains to see the world as it does. It can make powerful arguments (that's why it evolved). However, the Gut and the Heart did fine without it for millions of years, so they are inclined to ignore it when they disagree or think its contributions irrelevant.

Even so, the Head Brain is a powerful and persuasive cognitive engine. It is the finest learning and data-processing tool nature has ever produced. It can, at times, push the Heart Brain's priorities to the side and even, in more limited ways, persuade the Gut Brain to temper its reactions. But neither the Heart nor Gut Brains are so foolish as to let the Head, for all that cerebral horsepower, take charge. Neither Heart nor Head, in fact, can ever convince the Gut Brain to completely set aside its hard-wired programming. The times when the Heart or the Head Brains can override Gut Brain decisions are exceedingly rare.

> One extremely important quality the Head Brain has that the Heart and Gut Brain do not possess is the awareness of time. Why is this important? When the Heart or Gut are in charge, cause and effect analyses are not made. Meaning the Heart and Gut do not consider the consequences of their actions for the long run.

> If the Gut Brain had an awareness of cause and effect, we would eat differently and take care of the environmental issues, global warming etc.

Quite frankly, the Gut Brain and the Heart Brain don't speak the same language as the Head Brain. To communicate to the Gut, the Head Brain must use the language the Gut understands: emotions and feelings such as fear, anger, pain, need, desire. In most cases, the Heart Brain is far more powerful than the Head Brain. In fact, the Heart Brain is only inclined to listen to the Head Brain when it's on the fence about something and has no emotions invested. When it's certain about something — when its emotions are committed, it has no time for the Head Brain's nattering. Have you ever told yourself, "I really shouldn't love that person"? Did it work? Enough said.

The Head Brain knows how little influence it has on the Heart Brain. So, when it is convinced that the Heart Brain is making a mistake, it tries to enlist the Gut Brain to agree with it. If it does, the Heart might protest, but the Gut Brain can throw up roadblocks to the Heart Brain's reactions. You may feel sick about it (because it made you feel sick) — but Gut Brains usually get their way.

In fact, the Heart Brain, like the Head Brain, can modify the Gut's reactions — but only so much. If the Gut feels something is a safety issue, it will shut them both down and attend to its own priorities. This last statement, by the way, is no metaphor — the Gut Brain can turn off the other parts of your Brain if it thinks they are getting in the way. We will get back to this later.

The Head Brain's weakness — emotionally incompetent

There is an acronym that dates back to the dawn of computing: GIGO. It was used to explain why, sometimes, computers came up with the wrong answer — sometimes preposterously wrong. GIGO stands for 'Garbage In, Garbage Out'.

Your Head Brain is relentlessly seeking to understand how the world works. It looks for patterns, so it can make predictions. It generalizes, evaluates, and interprets information that is coming in. When it does, its owner can use that knowledge to better survive and prosper. But a Head Brain can only work with the information it gets. If you, or the people around you, feed it misinformation, wrong-headed notions, or weird superstitions, it can easily mistake them for reality and go on to make misinformed and foolish decisions.

Not only that, but once a Head Brain has fixed on an idea, it will rarely give it up — even, remarkably enough, when new and better information arrives. This willingness to ignore information that would require a person to reassess a fixed notion is a fundamental Head Brain weakness. It can cause havoc in our lives (and our political systems).

Mark Twain is often credited with a quotation that perfectly captures this Head Brain weakness: "It ain't what you don't know that gets you into trouble. It's what you know for sure that just ain't so."

SCIENCE NERD NOTE:

One of the writers I consulted on this book told me of an interview he did with Fred Haise, the lunar module pilot on the near disastrous Apollo 13 space mission. "What did it feel like, Mr. Haise, when the O2 tanks on your spacecraft exploded and you realized that your ship had lost almost all of its crucial air supply that you needed to stay alive?" "It felt like it was shaking. And I heard a kind of crinkling noise," he replied. Fred Haise survived that experience, because his Head Brain knew how to solve problems like that.

6.

How our Brains learn, decides how we act

Collectively, our Brains consume more than one-third of our daily energy; our Head Brain 24% by itself. Learning, and applying that learning, is its entire job. Clearly, Homo sapiens have placed a high priority on knowledge and insight. However different they are, all our Brains learn in the same two ways: First, by comparing an experience to things that have happened before, and second, if an experience seems novel, by creating physical connections and building pathways between the neurons.

If the new experience seems like something already learned, we associate the new experience with the old one. This process of 'association' — sorting the experience into a pre-existing category — is easy and requires little energy or effort. To save time and energy, it is always tried first.

When an experience appears to be entirely new, however, our Brains must create a totally new network of neural pathways. This is demanding work. It takes a lot of energy. Our Brains, therefore, only do this when they have no other choice. It's much easier to dump a new experience into a pre-made container, than to weave a whole new basket. In addition, too many containers slow down the process of thinking. Brains want to categorize things. It makes thinking about them easier. But, as you have no doubt surmised, we can make mistakes. When we do, when we start treating unlike things as like things, we create problems that are hard to unravel.

I'm sure you can think of dozens of examples in your own life, of times when you reacted to your boss or teacher like they were your parent, or to a colleague as if they were a kid you had a conflict with when you were in school. Sometimes, especially if the reaction is benign or the situation is in fact, similar — no problem. Other times, it can lead to a world of trouble. And situations like that are especially troublesome in relationships — where a person has an absolute right to be treated as an individual. If you have ever had anyone say to you, "I'm not your mother!" one of you has just made a big mistake in categories.

When all Three Brains are aligned and balanced out, and there is no domination of one over the others — that is a state of 'mindfulness' — it is the natural state of childhood and adulthood. But to get there, we sometimes need to clear out the things that get in our way.

BRAIN ALIGNMENT EXERCISE

One way to learn if we are really aligned and whether our Three Brains are cooperating is this simple exercise:

Sit in a comfortable position.

Inhale and exhale 30 times in circular breathing, meaning inhale for four seconds and directly exhale for four seconds (this will create heart coherence).

Become aware of what's happening in your mind and body.

If you are close to being in alignment, you may find thoughts popping up — small thoughts or things that still must be done — a small to-do list.

But if you find yourself feeling annoyed or anxious, worrying about big issues, that's a sign that your Three Brains are not aligned and disagree with one another.

If that happens, just follow these steps:

First breathe deeply, then exhale and imagine a heart-warming event.

Inhale, sending energy/light/warmth/love from your Heart to your Gut to assure it that all is safe.

Exhale, letting energy/light/warmth/love come up again into your Heart.

On the next inhale, send energy/light/warmth/love up to your Head from your Heart.

On the exhale, let the energy/light/warmth/love return to your Heart.

Do this a couple of times.

It's not a magic spell, but it does open channels of communication. You should notice that you have become less anxious and that the problems you are confronting seem to be ones you can solve, as your entire mind is now in action instead of one of the Brains.

Our Three Brains are invariably misaligned, to a lesser or greater degree. What has happened is that our different Brains have learned different things from our experiences. Even the same experience can be understood differently by our different Brains. Our conditioning/upbringing, painful negative or happy positive experiences are stored in our Gut, our Heart, and our Head Brains. Due to this misalignment, it can be hard to understand what is driving our own decision-making – much less that of someone else, with an entirely separate set of painful memories or moments of happiness.

When you think back to your parents and compare how your siblings would view them, how different are the viewpoints?

An extreme example of this is when someone is mentally, physically, or sexually abused. We have come to understand in recent years that such things are shockingly common.[28]

What do these experiences do to a person? And how do they come to influence their ability to make decisions later in life?

How to resolve the perspectives of your different Brains?

As we discussed above, when everything is working well, our Brains are working in harmony. However, the first thing we discussed about our Three Brains is that they experience the world and our environment in different ways and have entirely different strengths and weaknesses. Those different perspectives are all valuable, but learning how to resolve those differences is a skill that is far easier to do when you become truly aware of what each perspective is and then strive for a decision that addresses, or at least respects, the contribution of each. If you have established a healthy three-Brain relationship in your own thinking, you can be confident that, whatever you decide will be more likely to be successful.

If you have ever watched a relay race, you know the most important moment. Yes, the handover! It is the same with our Three Brains. When they work together, there is a perfect handover. If not, problems quickly follow.

The competition between them is likely to come to the fore when you are confronting an important life decision that looks very different when viewed through the lenses of safety and security (Gut Brain), emotional connections (Heart Brain) and logic, intellectual learning and understanding (Head Brain). One thing to be aware of is that this competition may or may not rise to the level of conscious awareness. If you are facing some big decision and are finding it hard to sleep, or are feeling anxious about it, that's a sign your Three Brains are wrestling with a decision that looks different to each of them and no solution has been found that all of them can accept.

One example of competing Brains is when you have an argument and there are always things you would like to say, but you hold your tongue. I am sure you have encountered multiple situations like this. Did you feel afterwards that you should have said something more, or differently, and you let the situation pass a couple of times through your mind, rewind it again and allow different outcomes?

This is when your Brains are competing. In this case, possibly, your Heart Brain was angry, but your Gut Brain put the brakes on for fear of getting fired or having to sleep on the couch.

Your Head Brain might be champing at the bit to point out how to do something better, but your Heart Brain advises you to zip it, because you don't want to bruise a loved one's feelings. Of course, your Gut Brain is the ultimate emergency brake. It abhors a fight — because fights are dangerous things. That's why, even if you do have a conflict, you will often feel a little sick afterwards. That's your Gut Brain telling you, "I told you so! Don't go doing that again!" The fact that you replay the scene a couple of times, and give it different outcomes, shows how the Head Brain likes to learn how to do it better next time.

The more difficult intra-cranial conflicts come when you are facing a decision that really impacts your life — like deciding to enlist in the army, or study abroad, or settle down with your hometown sweetheart, or contemplating spending more than you can afford on the car of your dreams.

How do your Brains resolve such a conflict? Here are some examples:

EXAMPLE: WHICH SCHOOL TO GO TO

One of my students at IE Business School in Madrid told me how she decided to go there from her home in India.

She said her Head had absorbed all it could about which business program was considered the best in the world, what other countries the students were coming from, and how the curriculum would equip her to work in the Western or Asian worlds. On the other hand, she was afraid her choice might be wrong, and she would never get the high-paying position she would need to pay her family back for supporting her while she studied.

Her Heart leaned toward business schools that attracted more Asians, so she would not feel isolated.

Her Head countered that going to such a school would not differentiate her from the pack when she was looking for a job after gaining her degree.

In the end, a high-ranking executive in her company recommended IE and promised her a job as soon as she returned with her MBA. With its fears of joblessness and penury taken care of, her Gut and Head Brains urged her to go to IE, and her Heart accepted their decision.

EXAMPLE: FINDING A PARTNER WITH ONLINE DATING

Nowadays, internet dating has made finding a match in a faraway town a common occurrence. But when you really want to put the idea into action and relocate for love, your Three Brains might not agree on the course.

Gut Brain: It's not likely to work out, you'll have to find a new job and you aren't so young anymore. The risks are just too high.

Heart Brain: "Faint heart never won fair lady." This is the love of your dreams! But, moving away from close friends and family? Hmm… that is hard!

Your Head Brain, of course, has conjured up a beautiful Excel spreadsheet with all the pros and cons of moving, the financial consequences, the practical consequences of going or staying… It would also run those same calculations for your new lover. Why are you the one who has to move? Does it make sense? And is his/her unwillingness to move, itself, a data point in itself? Maybe he/she isn't deeply committed.

At this point, the Gut Brain might step in and advise you to take care of yourself first. Which, of course, raises the question, "What is the best way to take care of yourself?" Since that could go either way, the argument will go around in circles until, most likely, the Gut Brain makes the decision itself, unless the Heart Brain really loves the challenge.

It's the noisy chatter of internal discussions like this that keep people awake during the night.

Section 3:

WHAT ARE PROS AND CONS OF A HEAD, HEART AND GUT BRAIN PARTNER?

7.

Gut Brain Partners: achievers, competitors, action oriented, and not the best for long lasting relationships

The good things about the Gut Brain (because it is an amazing Brain)

I can imagine that after you have read all the things about the Gut Brain you could ask yourself: why do we have a Gut Brain when it is not the best for long lasting relationships?

Easy, in the early days, when external threats surrounded us, instinctive survival was essential. Fear kept us alive, and our Gut Brain and the 'cerebellum' in our head, the little Brain on top of the brainstem at the top of the spine were 100% in charge. For survival reflexes, it did not even consult with us, and it still doesn't today.

The important thing about Gut Brain people is that they are the real survivors; when push comes to shove, they know how to survive. They are like the Avengers, Silvester Stallone in Rambo, Arnold Schwarzenegger in The Terminator, and Darth Vader in Star Wars. All these characters know how to get out of dangerous and life-threatening situations. The lust for life and for survival is all that counts.

For many people, a Gut Brain partner brings safety as they will protect the team (family) as long as their objective is the same as that of the team. In the old way of socialization, when women were expected to act helpless and submissive (only Heart Brain), they were forced to outsource their survival skills to a Gut Brain man.

And still nowadays, when one half of a couple has an underdeveloped survival Gut Brain, they have the tendency to seek a Gut Brain partner. This is specifically the case when the person also has a strongly developed Heart Brain. Why are the sugar daddies attractive, as for most of them they don't win any beauty contests! It is not their looks or physical health that makes them so attractive? Simple, they are providing financial safety.

'To survive' means that you must put your personal interest first. To be clear, it is never a Gut Brain's intention to hurt you or anyone else. It simply doesn't take you or anyone else into account. What happens to other people is immaterial to the goal of 'me-first' survival, unless they are the ones who pose the danger. In that case, they must be neutralized. This is not necessarily negative behavior as every gold medal winner at the Olympics and every serial entrepreneur has a strongly developed Gut Brain. You don't become a winner without a strong and dominant Gut Brain.

The best way to try and understand what drives Gut Brain people is to observe the origin of the Gut Brain. The answer is in our primitive animal ancestors, who were controlled and operated by their Gut Brain or survival instinct alone. Reptiles and some birds still only operate from the Gut Brain; some birds I like to advocate did develop a Heart Brain, think of 'social birds' like swans or crows. Observing their savage and self-centered behavior is a good lesson in showing us why we needed to evolve Heart and Head Brains to do more with our lives than just eat or be eaten.

But Gut Brain people, in a sense, are seagulls in human form. They are often blind to the fact that cooperation is a better strategy. Think of them as being like the greedy seagulls in the movie Finding Nemo. When presented with a chance to gulp down a fish, the gulls start squawking "Mine! Mine! Mine!"[29] They did not cooperate, and they all ended up with their beaks stuck in a sail and no fish.

When Gut Brains go bad: Misbehavior

One Gut Brain behavior that seems at odds with its focus on safety is misbehaving.

There are few things more viscerally irritating than the sound of a very loud motorcycle engine. It might come as a surprise that it's the showing off part from the Gut Brain that expresses, "I am strong, I am sexy," that is always gunning the throttle.

So, what's the thought process behind it? Like any Gut Brain behavior, it's not complicated. Aggressive behavior is one way of protecting yourself from potential threats. If you display that you are strong and tough, then you are protected. One thing is for certain, the person gunning the throttle of a loud motorcycle doesn't feel anywhere near as tough as they might seem.

Similarly, what do we think when we see someone flaunting their sexuality? That they are secure in their natural attractiveness? Probably not. More likely, we see someone who is afraid of being ignored.

As the Gut Brain is the most selfish part of you or anyone else, it is tremendously sensitive to anything that might become a safety problem — like a loss of status or being treated unfairly. The first thing to understand about people who are dominated by their Gut Brains is that it really is all about them. If you can also be all about them, you are welcome into their selfish world.

It always reminds me of a girlfriend I was once dating. In one moment, she said: enough about me, why don't you talk about me. Although it was said with a tongue in the cheek manner, it had a lot of truth in it!

Let's be frank. People who are dominated by their Gut Brains are no picnic. And they are everywhere. You can't escape them. Seven or eight of the next ten men that you pass on the street, and two or three of the next ten women, are at that moment dominated by the most selfish, aggressive, short-sighted, and stubborn of our Three Brains. Next time you walk to your work or school, just have a look around and observe the faces of the people on the street. Most of them are focused on going from A to B and are only thinking of getting there (Gut Brain) and not on interacting at all. And let's not mention when you are in public transport or in a café and people are totally 'Me' focused on their smartphone.

What messes up our Gut Brain? The question should be, "What doesn't?" Every upsetting experience we ever had, from bad parenting decisions, to misguided school discipline and negative stereotypes, are encoded into the Gut Brain's capacious, but unsophisticated, permanent memory. Every painful or traumatic memory of abusive bosses and schoolyard bullies join them there. No slight or humiliation is too small for the Gut Brain to keep hold of. Gut Brains only think in the present tense. A wound from decades ago feels as if it is happening right now.

If you ever felt that someone treated you unfairly, or if anyone ever betrayed your trust, you can count on your Gut Brain to remember and viscerally react to anything that reminds them of that feeling of powerlessness or insecurity. Gut Brains never let bygones be bygones. Bygones are ever-present wounds to the Gut Brain. If you trigger it in someone else, their Gut Brain cannot distinguish between you and the Grade 3 bruiser who humiliated them in a schoolyard scuffle. This is not to say that Gut Brains can't be taught to make that distinction. We will deal with how to civilize your own and other people's Gut Brains later in Section 5–The 8 rules of dealing with Gut Brains: take it safe.

So how can you recognize and, hopefully, defang the Gut Brain people in your life? How does a Gut Brain-dominated person communicate or behave? Anger, aggression, a focus on personal gratification and a lack of subtlety or sophistication are the hallmarks of Gut Brain behavior. Road rage? Gut Brain. An inappropriately aggressive response to a minor issue? Gut Brain. They are neither subtle nor measured in their reactions. To a Gut Brain, every need or fear is a no-holds-barred emergency.

What makes things worse is that Gut Brains have no way to distinguish small issues from large ones. As far as it is concerned, everything is life or death. Imagine you have treated yourself to a beautiful (and expensive) new jacket. It's an extravagance, but worth the price. When you bring it home, it does not go well. Your partner turns nasty, accusing you of wasting money, of not thinking about what else that money could have bought. Bingo! Your partner's Gut Brain felt danger and it counterattacked. Your new jacket has become a matter of life or death.

The Gut Brain's main objective is the opposite of a healthy relationship

So, the main objective of the Gut Brain is a lust for life. Self-preservation, the protection and safety of self is totally connected, and by extension, the instinctive desire to reproduce. It is the ultimate and perfect "me, myself and I" Brain.

To fulfill the main objective, lust for life or survival, the Gut can produce neurotransmitters and hormones that will evoke 7 sensations or emotions to drive our actions:

1. Desire
2. Lust
3. Fear (anxiety)
4. Anger
5. Rage
6. Hunger
7. Disgust (when connected with the Heart Brain, it could become hate)

I think we can agree that all of these are strong emotions and they should be. Survival is the highest-stakes game there is.

I think we all experience some of those sensations in our daily lives. Did you ever succeed to think yourself out of it in the moment? Probably not and that is the objective! It is 500 million years of experience to make you survive. But they are not the ones that should be in play when the objective is to share, nurture and connect.

For the moment, let's look more deeply into the things that drive Gut Brain thinking.

RELATIONSHIP EXAMPLE: RACING IN THE STREETS — A GUT BRAIN CONFLICT

Scene: You are in the passenger seat. A friend or your partner is at the wheel. They are driving fast. The world outside is a blur. You get nervous, then alarmed. You grip the door handle. Your palms are moist with sweat. Your Gut Brain is alerting you to danger and preparing you to do something to get to safety.

So, what tone of voice are you going to use to tell your friend or partner to slow down? Would you feel calm and at ease, full of love and understanding of the need to drive like a Formula One driver? Or would you snap? Would you go so far as to say, "Slow down! Are you trying to kill us you stupid?" (Hint: Gut Brains are not filled with soft words of love or understanding.)

When we talk about understanding how we fit with our partners, it becomes quite important to understand which one of our Brains is in the figurative driver's seat — the Gut, Heart or Head. Next, we need to understand which one our partner has put in charge.

In the above example, how did you figure out that the speed was too high?

Was it data from your Head Brain? Did you do the math? Did you note that you passed a lamp post every ½ second, and that they were each 25 meters apart? Did you then calculate 25x7200/1000 to conclude that the speed had to be 180 km/hour?

Or was it a disturbing feeling in your gut after seeing the lamppost passing by at rather high speed or maybe feeling pushed down in your seat?

It was your gut feeling. No question about it.

When safety is the issue, the Gut Brain does not need the math to make a decision it just takes over when it senses it should. That's the home of our survival instincts. The Head may be the home of quadratic equations, but the Gut Brain is incredibly good at calculating odds and counting. Too fast? Survival odds dropping? Gut Brain. Too many enemies to tangle with? Gut Brain. So, it was your Gut Brain that sensed the speed and did its own reckoning. Within a tenth of a second, it sounded the alarm, "Danger! Danger! Danger!"

When the Gut Brain reacts, it does not use words. Its tools are to signal to upstairs to the Heart and Limbic brain to go on full alert (read more about this in the science of the Three Brains and the SAM and HPA axes) and the hormones and neurotransmitters are released to prepare your body for handling danger. Your hands instinctively reach for something to hold onto. Your heart beats faster. Your breathing increases. Your gut was preparing your body to do battle or skedaddle — more commonly known as 'fight or flight'.

A few seconds afterwards the neocortex part of your Head Brain catches up.

The question here is: What do you do to feel safe again? And which of your Brains handles the communication? Do you gasp and scream? If the danger is immediate, your Gut Brain will do just that — long before the other Brains can weigh in.

If there is time, the Heart and Gut Brains will analyze what is happening and which Brain should be consulted to react appropriately.

The thing to remember here is that we feel or sense first (Gut and Heart Brains) and only later does the Head Brain weigh in with its store of learned facts and intellectual experience. So, our Heart and Gut Brains are the first responders to any of our feelings, and then our Head Brain is providing suggestions for the actions we could take.

When we feel safe, the Head Brain can act quickly. When I ask you a simple question like, "What is 2 + 2?" you can answer me without even giving it a second thought.

When we are in an unsafe environment, for instance, when we're walking down a dark alley with strange-looking people around, or we're driving at 200 km/hour, even the simplest of mathematics like 2+2 seems hard to do.

In an environment that the Gut Brain feels is unsafe, it takes control and places all its energy and focus on surviving. Is doing math a basic need for survival right now? No. So, the Gut Brain walls off all input from the Head Brain and the Heart Brain until the perceived crisis is over.

Desire and lust, without them there is no life

Think back to when you met your partner for the first time — that first second when you made contact — can you really say that physical attraction and desire were nowhere to be found?

When you are hungry or thirsty and see that amazing cake, coffee, or whatever, you have an amazing craving for it and cannot hold yourself back from it. In that moment that is lust and desire.

But there is one thing to be very aware of when it comes to physical desire. Your Gut Brain is supplying it. And it is fully capable of switching off our Head Brain's rationality and our Heart Brain's emotional connections. Lust is powerful, irrational, and selfish. It can get the best, and very often the worst out of us as we know from the obesity epidemic binge drinking, the '#MeToo' revelations, to all the rapes carried out in war zones and pitifully also in domestic life. Desire and Lust are extremely powerful impulses.

The lust to reproduce stops the Head Brain from reasoning and stops the Heart Brain from feeling.

As you may have seen in documentaries about the black widow spider, for the male, mating is an infamously dangerous activity. The larger females will often eat the smaller males as a dessert after sex — hence her honorary name of 'widow'. In many cases, the female catches the male while he's trying to escape.

Similarly, a male praying mantis will be eaten alive during the mating process. In most cases, the female bites off his head, then devours his corpse for nourishment.

Now back to you: would you take the risk of having sex if you knew you would be eaten or killed afterwards? Probably not, but can you remember those moments when you were in that state? Were you thinking of what else you should do, from shopping to the stressful presentation you have to deliver the day after?

Do you remember that amazing song of Meatloaf, paradise by the paradise light?

She: Will you love me forever?

He: Let me sleep on it

She: Will you love me forever!

He: I couldn't take it any longer
Lord I was crazed
And when the feeling came upon me
Like a tidal wave
I started swearing to my god and on my mother's grave
That I would love you to the end of time
I swore that I would love you to the end of time!
So now I'm praying for the end of time
To hurry up and arrive

'Cause if I gotta spend another minute with you
I don't think that I can really survive

So, even though the outcome is unhappiness for the rest of our life (according to Meatloaf) or death, the instinctive lust to reproduce is greater than the perceived danger or sacrifice. We all have something of that deep inside our Gut Brain DNA.

Although we humans have a much more developed nerve and brain system, this primary strong emotion of lust is still there, and has the capacity to pitifully overrun the logical Head Brain or the feeling Heart Brain. This is especially true if we did not develop those two Brains during our early lives in order to make a more balanced decision. When we have a well-developed Heart Brain, this lack of balance happens less often.

Example: Finding her way

I once had a female client in her early 40s with three young children. She had been with her husband for more than 20 years, having met him when she was 18. She had gone to an all-girls school and never really knew any men before she met her partner. She told me she didn't know how to talk to men when she left school and the first boy who made her feel loved she stayed with. Two decades later, her husband was leaving her for a younger woman, and she felt bereft. "I missed all those fun years," she lamented.

She went on Tinder and had some fun dates, just to experience how it is to have other men in bed, to have breakfast, and then move on. She told me, "I missed that part of my life so now I deserve it to have it."

This is the Gut Brain competing with the Heart Brain and the logical Head Brain.

For me it is not about whether she was right or wrong in what she was doing, it is more that she needed to be aware of whether or not one of the Brains was actually taking control in competing with the others and that in the long run it would not cause damage, guilt or trauma in one of her other Brains.

In Survival mode there is no time for relationships

The Gut Brain means well. If it thinks money is an issue, it rises to defend the family coffers. But Gut Brains don't know how to be nice about it. Who has time for nice in an emergency like this?! We know now that the Gut Brain has three go-to reactions to increase the odds of survival:

- Fear
- Anger/rage
- Paralysis (Surrender: the last resort)

Where these emotions make sense, of course, is when you really are in a life-threatening situation. Unfortunately, they can also be fired up for far lesser reasons, for example, if there are disagreements within your social group, or if your partner seems to be flirting with someone else. Even if it is for only a millisecond, the Gut Brain will scan if what he/she is saying to the other person or what he/she is saying to him/her could pose a danger to you or not. If the Gut Brain thinks that an interest of yours is being threatened, it will provoke anger — or even escalate to rage, with a view to protecting you and your relationship.

So how do you cope with a partner's hair-triggered Gut Brain reaction? If you are afraid your partner will fly off the handle about pricey purchases, you will avoid such confrontations. You could give in and not buy anything like it ever again. You might hide such purchases or expenses. If the Gut Brain was right about the expense, and it really was irresponsible, then maybe not buying things like it again is reasonable. But if it was a controlling overreaction, then some retraining (or a new partner) is the better solution. (Lying about it might buy you some time but sets you up for even worse when the lie is exposed.)

If you feel strong enough to handle and win this fight (your own Gut Brain response), or your values are so strong that you believe you did right by following your other Brains (your Heart Brain), then in most cases you will pick up the glove and go for the discussion/fight to prove you are right in what you did. This does not mean your partner will back off, more that you don't back off. The result depends on how well both of you go from a fight (Gut Brain) to a healthy discussion (Heart and Head Brain).

If whatever you are doing that provokes a Gut Brain response from your partner is not something that is important to you, your Heart Brain will advise you to simply stop doing it. If it is important, or you are feeling bullied, then you need to resolve, not avoid, the issue.

When your Three Brains are well aligned, and you think and feel that you're able to deal with your partner's behavior that is directed from his/her Gut Brain, then you first need to figure out what fear is triggering their reaction. You are then in a better position to defuse it. On the other hand, when you are afraid your partner might fly off the handle over any expense at all, then your Gut Brain will make its decision based on fear and YES, that is a sign of a deeply troubled relationship.

One thing to know about interacting with someone else's Gut Brain: it's not really a job your Head Brain can succeed at. No one's Gut Brain thinks logically, and Gut Brains are loath to listen to their own Head Brains. They are certainly not interested in hearing from someone else's. The best bet in this kind of situation is to wait until the Gut Brain deactivates. Then, possibly, you can connect on the level of your Head or Heart Brains – a conversation based on logic and the importance of emotional connection. If you can do that, then, maybe, their Head or Heart Brains can have a much-needed intra-cranial conversation with their own Gut Brain and convince it to lighten up a bit. You will notice that I peppered those last statements with uncertainties. You may, or may not, persuade your partner this way. But the odds are much better than trying to reason with someone else's Gut Brain. That never works.

Rage is so useful until it is not

In the old days, we humans were hunter-gatherers and we were prey for other predators. The gut instinct to survive, protect against predators and to kill/steal prey was the most important thing of all. We needed to run as fast as possible when in danger, and we had to fight to save our lives when we could not run or escape. In that situation, rage is extremely useful. It can override fear and every animal uses anger/rage as protection.

I think all of us have had an experience somewhere in the past when we were in such a rage, we said and did things without thinking of the consequences. When we cooled down, we might have been embarrassed or felt guilty about it. But what happened is simply how the system works: The Heart and Head Brains get switched off when we are in a rage. When we are in that extreme 'fight' mode, the blood flow to the neocortex — the Head Brain — is diverted to deliver its energy to the muscles of the chest, arms and lungs.

If you have ever watched one of those war movies/series, like Saving Private Ryan, The Water Diviner, Dunkirk or Game of Thrones, you see combatants doing things in a total rage. If the Head Brain or Heart Brain would have stepped in, they would have never done those things to a human being. Thinking logically with your Head or Heart while you're crushing somebody else's head, or putting a knife in someone's throat, is not helpful. It will make you start doubting your actions and before you know it, you will be dead.

It is a good thing that very few of us live inside the plots of war movies. But we carry with us a Gut Brain that is always ready to go berserk if it feels it needs to. The challenge, for most of us, is to devise ways to keep our Gut Brains feeling safe. If we don't, fear (anxiety) and anger will be part of our life 24/7. That's a hard life to live — and an impossible one for our loved ones and partners.

The beauty of Hunger and disgust

In 1943, researcher Maslov wrote that the first needs that must be met are the primary survival needs: Breathing, food and water.[30]

Naturally, we do our absolute best to avoid emotions like hunger/thirst, and their protective sibling, disgust. Disgust is there to protect us, so that we don't eat or drink something toxic or rotten.

You can also be disgusted about what somebody else is doing. How many times have you said about something that is happening, "It really makes me want to vomit." There you have the emotion of disgust in action, originating from your Gut Brain.

This hunger/thirst emotion is strong in our daily life. Think about the last time you went out for lunch and visited the supermarket before eating. Didn't all those sugary snacks look irresistible?

Our brain works on glucose, it loves sugar, and our Gut Brain knows that. Most supermarkets capitalize on this need and entice you with sugary snacks next to the checkout counter. Just observe how many people will grab one, even when they have already had lunch.

What we eat, why we eat, how we eat, and the desire for food explains another part of us. Beside the sugar craving, it's also about how we use food to nurture ourselves. It makes the Gut Brain feel good when it's supplied with food.

Why do you think business meetings are often lunch or dinner meetings? It makes the Gut Brains feel happy, so it is much more likely to lead to a positive result.

Example: A Gut Brain relationship

In my therapy room, one of the couples had relationship issues. They initially said they had issues with the differences in how each wanted to live their life. When I questioned them more, and asked what had made them fall in love with each other, they both responded, "The sex!" Now it was the sex that was becoming an issue. The man said that he felt like his partner was not attractive anymore — and he feared that their relationship would end. His partner agreed: the issues they had previously were always solved in the bedroom. Now that the sex was infrequent, their other differences became more irritating and disturbing. This is a situation where their relationship was built on the Gut Brain, and the other Brains were not involved.

How are the lusty parts of our Gut Brain leading us into trouble? We are driven by physical desires that are untampered by our Heart Brain's need for emotional connection and the Head Brain's understanding of consequences.

How does this work? Recently, I was walking in the forest thinking about this book, and a beautiful example was presented to me by two teenage boys and a teenage girl. They were sitting at a table and one of the boys was showing off, making strange movements, saying strange things in an odd voice.

I was excited to see this example thrown at my feet of how a lot of teenage boy's act. This is a typical Gut Brain response from the reproductive part of our Gut Brain. For some odd reason, teenage boys think that if they do crazy things, the other sex will be impressed. And, sometimes, it does work, because it makes the girl laugh. Many women will say that they like a man who can make them laugh, because it opens the social Heart Brain connection – ventral vagal nerve – and therefore the release of endorphins. I have heard many times in my therapy room that humor in a man can definitely be more attractive than conventional good looks. A 'boring' handsome man is rarely seen as attractive. I wonder what your thoughts are about that statement, as attractiveness is more a Gut Brain interest.

For a really impressive example of a male showing off to a female, look no further than the tiny Japanese puffer fish. The male builds a three-me-ter-wide sand sculpture on the featureless seabed, by using his fins to dig furrows.[31] He works day and night for up to two weeks, in the hope that his artwork will attract a female mate. (The female puffer fish are apparently attracted to the grooves and ridges as it shows a well-developed Gut Brain mechanism and fish go more for survival than love).[32]

Or think of peacocks, whose beautiful (and hard-to-manage) feathers have evolved simply to fire up the lusty synapses of peahens.

In the human world, we go to the gym to tone our bodies, we dress to impress, we take foolish risks. All this to make us appear good virile, or fertile, mating material. Men and women both do it, sometimes in different ways. When you look at dating sites, you can see such posing in action. Men try to appear tough and smart, women warm and smart. And everyone wants to appear in top physical shape, as the Gut Brain has a slightly faster reaction time than the Heart and Head Brains.

Don't get me wrong, it is totally normal and healthy to do your best to attract a mate. And having someone who is clearly trying to appeal to you is, in itself, attractive. It is only an issue when they get stuck in this behavior, when it becomes the normal way of living. When you disregard your own well-being to impress, then the Gut Brain's desire has taken over — to the detriment of emotional or intellectual connections.

A little advice: if you meet someone — male or female — who needs constant validation and always needs to impress, don't doubt just run.

In some people, lust can completely disable the logical mind from reasoning and the heart from feeling. When you think about evolution and survival, it does make sense that men and women behave differently in this one aspect of life. As far as copulation goes, men can afford to think less of consequences. Women, as the ones who can get pregnant, are more likely to consult their Head Brain. In addition, women are more likely to be endangered in sexual situations. As a result, their Gut Brain's need to assert power for safety — even over its own physical desire.

And it is never an excuse for any men or women to say, "Well, this is just what I am and what I am built for." We all do possess a Heart Brain and a Head Brain and can learn to use them when making decisions. And yes, they are mostly a result of socializing and stereotyping. Let's not forgot it is not gender defined, there are many women and men who will use their appearance to get what they want.

How the Gut brain overturns the strongest belief: religion

Let's look at scientific proof of how the Gut Brain will overrule the Heart Brain when there is a choice between compassion and following a selfish objective, even though the students of the Theological Seminary of Princeton, who carried out the research, said the results can be explained by compassion. When I read this example in Malcolm Gladwell's The Tipping Point, I was puzzled.[33]

Two Princeton University psychologists, John Darley and Daniel Batson, wanted to find out if people who study the good of humanity, and who dedicate their lives to that, would act in that way when challenged to choose between the Gut Brain and Heart Brain.

The main question was: "As the subjects study theology, would they behave in a way that demonstrates the theological principles of humanity, and choose to help another person (Heart Brain), or would they behave more selfishly and only care about their own objective (Gut Brain) if they had to choose between those two options?"

The research group of students were asked to prepare and deliver a presentation to another group of students. The presentation was supposed to be on a biblical theme. They had some time to prepare it, then they had to walk over to another building to present it.

There were two groups: one was not given enough time to reach the other building, the other one had enough time.

During the walk, they would run across a man, who was curled up with his head down, coughing and groaning, clearly in need of help.

What would the theological students do?

Would they listen to their Heart Brain and actually act on the content of their talk, namely stop and help the man, knowing that they would be late for the presentation? Or would they follow instructions from *the Gut Brain, taking on the 'me first' attitude, ignore the man and go directly to the presentation?*

To see if their beliefs would make a difference to the outcome, Darley and Batson introduced three variables into the experiment.

Before the experiment even started, they split into groups based on a questionnaire that asked them why they had chosen to study theology.

Was it for personal and spiritual fulfillment, or were they looking for a practical tool for finding meaning in everyday life? This was checking the Heart Brain connection.

After this, they introduced the topics for the presentation.

A neutral one: 'The relevance of the professional clergy to the religious vocation', and one that was all about the test: 'The parable of the Good Samaritan'. This was to determine if they had something to present about the good Samaritan, whether it would affect their behavior (as a story of the good Samaritan is all about this challenge they would face; to stop or not to stop to help).

The two topics were then shared across the two groups, creating four groups in total.

To create the time stress factor, the instructor sent the students on their way, while looking at his watch and saying, "Oh, you're late. They were expecting you a few minutes ago. You'd better get moving."

In other cases, he would say, "You still have time, it will be a few minutes before they're ready for you, but you may as well head over now."

So, who played the Good Samaritan?

Who do you think stopped for the man and who did not?

I assume we would all like to say that the students who entered the ministry to help people (Heart Brain) and who were also reminded of the importance of compassion by having just read the parable of the Good Samaritan (Heart Brain), would be the most likely to stop.

Here comes the beauty of the Gut Brain and Heart Brain, and how they show their real nature in deciding and communicating.

Surprisingly, neither of those factors made any difference.

Darley and Batson concluded, "It is hard to think of a context in which norms concerning helping those in distress are more salient than for a person thinking about the Good Samaritan, and yet it did not significantly increase helping behavior."

You would laugh if you saw it in a comedy show: "On several occasions, a seminary student going to give his speech on the parable of the Good Samaritan literally stepped over the victim as he hurried on his way."

The real difference between those who stopped and provided help and those who did not, was the perception of the students of how late they were.

10% of the group that was late stopped to help, while of the group that had enough time to spare, more than 60% stopped to help.

The words "Oh, you're late," had the effect of turning on the survival part of the Gut Brain; the fear of being rejected or judged was enough to activate the survival mechanism and turn off the compassionate Heart Brain.

Gut Brain domination: Run, fight or freeze

When the Gut Brain dominates, it's always on alert and ready to activate the sympathetic nervous system for the fight or flight response — or, sometimes, the opposite: a person could become depressed and lose their delight in life. Soldiers in combat have a Gut Brain that is on 24/7 alert, stock exchange traders the same.

To solve this 'stress" for the Gut Brain it is common that people who have a Gut Brain domination, have the tendency to be controlling, bossy, can't say sorry, won't show vulnerability, often show a lack of empathy and definitively show it is my way of the high way attitude.

Another example of what can happen when a Gut Brain is traumatized is when a person is raised in an environment that has taught them that their only role is to please those around them. Their normal default Gut Brain state is surrender, shock and self-denial. And, together with their traumatized Heart Brains, they come to conflate safety with love. This is something that often happens to women who have been raised to think of themselves only as enablers of the men around them, without an independent will and potential of their own.

Pitifully persons who have these traits often have a relationship with a Gut Brain dominant partner, the Gut Brain partner is totally happy with a submissive partner and the submissive partner finds "safety" and.........

DOMESTIC VIOLENCE IS PITIFULLY ALL TOO COMMON.

If you find yourself in a relationship in which your partners Gut Brain wants to make all their relationship decisions and wants to control what you are doing, that's a sign that the interactions you are having are, or could become emotionally (or even physically) unsafe. It's time to either do some serious behavior modification or to get out of the relationship as soon as possible.

Should You Avoid Gut Brain People Altogether?

You can't. They are everywhere. And they are not all bad. It's not like they don't have Heart Brains or Head Brains. It's just that, in their world, they feel anxious and constantly in danger. Once they feel safe, and their Heart Brains and Head Brains can become active, Gut Brain people can become delightful people. Depending on the person, and how deep the level of Gut Brain-driven self-preservation is embedded, this may require a little work — or it may be next to impossible.

It is not my intention to scare you with all these revelations about the Gut Brain and make you run away the moment you consider connecting with a partner who is dominated by their Gut Brain. But it is wise to keep a bit of distance. Don't try to save them from themselves. Becoming fully human is their responsibility, not yours, and anyway, their Gut Brain wouldn't let you. It would just turn your good intentions into self-gratification. What do they say about people who ride on tigers? They end up inside.

However, they need to be really willing to work on this, to clean up the mess, to forgive themselves for letting this interfere so much and for such a long time in their life. They need to forgive everyone who contributed to the pain, and to educate their Heart Brain, so that they can return to a healthy balance across their Three Brains.

So, look closely with your Heart Brain to see if there is a connection that can be nourished, so it will grow. Now that you can recognize Gut Brain behavior and communication, you can determine if a connected relationship is possible. If it is, you can open the door to love and intimacy. But if it is not, any relationship you have will turn you into a satisfier of someone else's needs. Sooner or later, your Head or your Heart Brains will rebel — but, if it's later, you will have done yourself some damage. Or, even before that, the Gut Brain person will have chosen their gratification over your relationship — and you will be left with a broken heart.

When your friends say someone is bad news, they are usually right. However, you have nothing to worry about as you are now aware of how their minds work. In the section, Connecting the dots, we dive further into recognizing Gut Brain people, and how to communicate with them.

Without the Gut we would not be here, and with only a Gut Brain active, we act the same as the seagulls.

A Scene in a Gut Brain's day

You are sitting on the couch talking to your partner. You begin to feel like you are talking to a wall.

"Are you are listening to me?"

Your partner responds, "Huh?"

The next day, you are in the supermarket going over what to buy. Again, your partner seems to be somewhere else.

What is going on here is the Gut Brain is dominating his or her actions, maybe with an activated Head Brain. And Gut Brains are not social creatures. As we well know by now, Gut Brains are all about their needs and their safety.

Let's look at another example. You are talking to a colleague about a project. They seem oblivious.

"Did you hear what I was saying?"

"Not really. I am not responsible for that project; this is your issue."

Here are the kinds of things we say when our Gut Brain is doing the talking: "I am stronger, better, more good-looking, smarter, braver, more individualistic and tougher. I have more friends than you or anyone else." In fact, almost everything related to competition is directed from the Gut Brain. To the Gut Brain, competition is a fight and a way of living. So, a word that the Gut Brain does not know is 'sorry'. A true Gut Brain will never say sorry, that would mean showing vulnerability or real interest in the other person. So, to expect the response "I am sorry" is a no go.

Once a client shared with me after her horrible divorce that her ex-husband who had the traits we just described, "he said sorry to me once in 23 years of being together."

Fun Fact:

One place you can see Gut Brains in all their glory is when you are driving. The person who cuts you off to save two seconds of their commute: Gut Brain at the wheel.

A true masculinity stereotype is actually a walking, talking Gut Brain

In a lot of books, you will find the Gut Brain addressed and stereotyped as masculine. In our culture, young men are often raised to play the stereotypical (some would say "traditional") role of a strong, capable, competitive and determined man.

Not once in this book will you find Gut (or any other) Brain thinking described as masculine or feminine. Even so, if you are raised to become a stereotype, you either conform to it or pay a price. You think it is only you who is experiencing or dealing with these kinds of men. Absolutely not, just listen to Beyoncé's If I Were a Boy and you will get an idea of how we stereotype — and society defends — Gut Brain behavior as "manly":

> *If I were a boy*
> *Even just for a day*
> *I'd roll out of bed in the morning*
> *And throw on what I wanted and go*
> *Drink beer with the guys*
> *And chase after girls*
> *I'd kick it with who I wanted*
> *And I'd never get confronted for it*
> *Cause they'd stick up for me*
>
> *...*
>
> *I'd put myself first*
> *And make the rules as I go*

If someone can treat Beyoncé badly, no living soul is immune. Let's not start to blame men, and further the stereotype, that all of them are like this, because we all have a Gut Brain. Yes, men are more likely to be socially forgiven for Gut Brain behavior, but do not forget that at least 20–30% of women are dominated by their Gut Brains as well.

In the twenty-first century, in most Western countries, it has become more acceptable for women to make their own way in the world and make their own decisions. We may be a long way from true equality, but, for women, the risk of being cast out of society for behavior that used to be considered 'masculine' is lower than it once was.

Society is no longer so strict in enforcing rules that prescribe what a woman should or should not do (even if many still hold onto such outdated beliefs). In the business world, many women have taken powerful positions on executive boards and other jobs that require the relentless appetite for success or power of a Gut Brain-driven person. In sports, many formerly male-dominated sports, like soccer or rugby, now have ferociously competitive women's teams.

Has the Revolution arrived? That is beyond the scope of this discussion, so we will merely observe here that more and more people can now become who they want to be. Both boys and girls are now more inclined to be raised to believe that their possibilities are determined by talent and drive, rather than by gender.

8.

Heart Brain partners: connecting, loyal, self-sacrificing and it is always about "us"

Heart Brain people are true loyal partners, they don't go for the outside they go for your inside.

"Do you love me?"

"Of course, why would you ask that?"

"Because you don't say it so often, and last time when I asked you if you liked cuddling up on the coach together, you responded, 'That's uncomfortable. I'm watching television now'. That feels so cold to me."

"Wow, that's a big jump from not sitting together on a couch to you thinking I do not love you anymore. What's wrong with you?"

So, what the Gut Brain or the Head Brain could think of as major assumptions or jumps from one point to another, is what a Heart Brain person feels as a normal way of communication; they are the empaths of this world and love connection.

Heart Brain people love to connect and act mostly without being bothered by logic or fears, like the saying "love is blind". They are hopeful in relationships — sometimes against all odds — that it will work out well. They will sacrifice their own needs to make that happen. They are also seen as the extremely sensitive people who feel how it is with you and want to connect with you.

Heart Brain people are the connectors, they love to have connection, to feel appreciated, and they really dislike rejection. They are the experts in creating a connection and feeling the connection with others.

To get a picture in your mind of what real 100% Heart Brain people are like, just watch Hachi: A Dog's Tale.[34] Hachiko the dog met his owner at the train station every day after work and continued to go to the train station every day for nine years, even after his owner passed away.

Heart Brain emotions, the connection builders

Heart Brain people are directed by an emotional compass, based on four main streams of emotions:

- Connecting:

    - Love
    - Hope
    - Acceptance
    - Compassion

- Optimism

    - Joy
    - Happiness

- Reconnection

    – Guilt
    – Shame
    – Sadness

- Protection

    – Aversion
    – Hate

All the above are emotions that are rooted in the bonds between people. For Heart Brain people, it is about 'Us' and not about 'Me'.

The emotions of love, hope , acceptance and compassion all have in common the traits of bonding and connection. They are closely connected with happiness and joy. They demonstrate the optimistic world view of all is good, I am okay and you're okay. Just think of that little baby with that big smile and laugh looking at you.

Whilst guilt, sadness and shame are at play when there is a disconnection, we do not like to feel these emotions, which promotes us to reconnect. If those sensations are guilt or shame it is perceived that we have done something wrong and breached some values or rules, causing us to be expelled from the group.

Finally, aversion and hate are there to protect 'Us' when somebody has done something 'wrong' and the Heart decides it is the best to be disconnected from that person. These emotions do the work of cutting the ties.

The scientific research shows the Heart Brain secretes neurohormones, such as dopamine and norepinephrine, that make a person feel happy and content. The Heart Brain (along with the Head Brain) also secretes oxytocin — the love or bonding hormone.

The Heart Brain and its emotions create empathy, sympathy, sacrifice, nurturing, and caring for another and their needs.

It is quite common for someone with a strong Gut Brain to have an equally powerful Heart Brain. Think of Marlon Brando's character in The Godfather — brutal to outsiders, but tender to his own. In a later movie in that franchise, Al Pacino dies from a broken heart after his daughter is shot. If you think about it, the root of clannishness and xenophobia is a powerful Heart Brain connection that loves insiders but hates outsiders. That, in turn, teaches the Gut Brain to treat outsiders as threats.

In fact, the Gut Brain does its best to protect the Heart Brain whenever it can – in matters large and small.

HEART BRAIN PEOPLE: THE EXTERNAL SOURCE FOR OUR SELF-ESTEEM AND CONFIDENCE

We need a Heart Brain supporter to instill self-esteem and self-confidence in us. I remember when I took my swimming exam and had to swim nine meters underwater. I was nine years old and all the parents were watching us. I was so nervous that I forgot to take a breath before diving in and did not achieve the full length; I came up after six meters.

I was almost crying, and saw my dad going to the examiners and talking to them. They let me have a second go. I was so afraid to fail again that I swam 20 meters underwater, too afraid to come up again and disappoint my father. I was also so afraid at being laughed at by the other parents that I almost drowned myself!

The compassionate Heart Brain action from my dad, who totally believed in me, allowed me to succeed and achieve

There are multiple examples of people receiving 100% trust and compassion, and achieving miraculous success. Edison would never have been the inventor he turned out to be if his mother had not completely supported him and provided him trust and compassion. She labelled him as a success even though the entire school board and teachers were against him and perceived him as a moron.[35] And again, that was when he was a child/teenager, not an adult.

Important to know is that our Three Brains are all connected and work together. We are an highly developed integrated system, the result the Gut Brain is acting many times as a big protective brother of sister for the Heart:

Let's say you pose a question like: "Why did you choose that dress?" or "Why did you do that?"

Even if the asking was innocent, it is likely to be taken as a criticism and you can get a slap back if the hearer's Heart has been bruised in the past by being judged and rejected.

So, what happens?

The Gut Brain, sensing that the Heart feels unsafe, will take over the instant something smells, looks or sounds like a judgment or rejection and will respond with avoiding or attacking response.

So, when we communicate with Heart people, it is good to make sure, above all else, that they feel safe with you. Otherwise, their Gut Brain might just bite your head off.

Whilst writing this second version he revenge song of Shakira about her ex-husband Piquet just broke all the Spotify records, a "nice" example of a Gut Brain talking over.

Heart Brain people they have a tendency for trying to heal damaged people … to their own detriment

Depending on your point of view, the fact that Heart Brains have an affinity for people who need to be healed is either a charm or a weakness. In fact, it is both. Caring for one another, tending to the very young and very old, and nursing the ailing is what we call 'humanity'. However, especially if we are insecure, those caring instincts can draw us to people who are damaged. I focus on insecurity here because it is often more than just compassion that drives people to find broken people who need fixing. It is sometimes, a feeling that someone who comes to depend on you is much less likely to reject you. If you have built yourself into their support system, they can't afford to let you go.

If you are one of those people who have had a series of relationships with people who needed your love and support, but who were incapable of returning it to you in equal measure, you need to fire up your Gut Brain to make sure you are not burning up your own candles. I have seen too many clients/patients who are amazing people but who were excusing their abusive partner.

I had a really dear friend who cannot share her story anymore as she has been shot by her partner before he shot himself. In the beginning of their relationship, it was the typical Gut Brain attraction, he was a typical cool good-looking firefighter and based on his troubled youth he showed the typical controlling, egocentric Gut Brain behavior and it came later to the surface that he also had shown some violent behaviors with one of his ex-partners.

Although she also had a well-developed Gut Brain, she also had a soft spot in her Heart for people who were in a state of helplessness. As their relationship moved on, he became depressed after he had to leave the fire brigade and he had gone on medication after an attempted suicide. He started to isolate himself and started to make a hill out of every molehill. She supported him as well as she could. The house of cards crashed however when she was diagnosed with an autoimmune disease. His wiring snapped with horrible consequences. Luckily this doesn't happen in all such cases but even one is one too many.

That said, there is something appealing about rule-breakers and rebels — as long as they are not also exploiters, they can be wonderful partners. It's just worth figuring out early on what they are rebelling against, and what they stand for.

The movie Grease is built around a familiar trope that has been around since the dawn of storytelling: good girl meets bad boy (who is really a good boy underneath). When the good girl and the bad boy have a summer holiday fling, he is gentle and kind. Thinking they will never see each other again; they end up in the same high school. Olivia Newton-John has moved to his high school where he is the bad boy following his Gut Brain's advice. Shocked that he is not the same boy she met on holiday, she sings the song Hopelessly devoted to you.

> "My head is saying, fool forget him
> My heart is saying, don't let go
> Hold on to the end, that's what I intend to do
> I'm hopelessly devoted to you
> But now there's nowhere to hide
> Since you pushed my love aside
> I'm outta my head, hopelessly devoted to you"

Logically, it does not make sense to want to have a relationship with the bad boy, but the heart sometimes likes to rescue the bad boy and bring out the good that the Heart thinks or likes to see inside that person. Sometimes the Heart Brain person cannot imagine that people do not have a heart, and they would love to see the heart behind the person's exterior character. Sadly, they think that by giving them enough love and attention, that person will change from a Gut Brain person to a Heart Brain person. The truth is that the only people in whom we can create that change are babies and children; they rarely have a messed-up Gut Brain that is turned on 24/7. Even if they have, we can, based on their development, change so much (see more in Section 6: **For when you have Children, how do their Three Brains work?**)

When we look at the positive emotions of the Heart Brain — love, hope, joy, happiness, acceptance, and compassion — it makes sense that there is a trust and belief that people can change, and that the bad boy can turn into a good boy. When you connect love to hope, acceptance, and compassion, you find the reason why this is happening.

When the Heart Brain is not properly connected and communicating, and not listening to the Gut Brain and Head Brain, it is going to be a mess. Our Three Brains evolved so that they can work together. If they work independently, the result is usually painful.

This is where it goes mostly wrong in relationships. The Heart Brain sees the possibilities for the union, although logically it does not make sense. In this kind of relationship, you're the therapist or 'mother' of your partner, and this will result in a dead-end for 99% of cases. It is sadly true that if you don't succeed as the therapist of your partner, you only hurt yourself, and when you do a great job as their therapist, it usually also results in pain. After they are cured, they will often run away with somebody else because they do not need you anymore.

Heart Brain people are the team builders

I was sitting on the beach, looking for inspiration. Next to me was a young family with a three-month-old child. For two hours, I watched as mom and dad cuddled the child and took hundreds of pictures. Every burp was documented for posterity. I felt like I was on a Heart Brain safari. In that moment, there was no selfish Gut Brain activity, only a loving and caring Heart Brain family group.

Forming such groups is the reason we developed Heart Brains in the first place. For successful life in families and groups, that emotional, limbic Brain was needed to process and regulate the emotions sent out by the Gut Brain and Heart Brain. We needed to make intelligent decisions about what was good for the group and what was not. To make such decisions, the Heart Brain needs (without being bothered about all the other emotions of the Gut Brain) to consult the Head Brain, which contributes its experiences and future predictions to make a decision.

In the workforce, the Heart Brain-rooted emotional skill of collaboration, working in teams, is essential for success. It's the same in team sports, a high-functioning collaborative team can usually beat a team of selfish stars. That's why a lot of coaches do not want a prima donna (a Gut Brain activity, because for a prima donna it's about him or her only) on the roster.

Heart Brain people are the courageous ones

When we come back to the emotions that are more connected to the heart, I said that the main ones that direct connection are: Love, hope, joy, happiness, acceptance, and compassion.

There is one special emotion or feeling unexpectedly not on the list: 'courage'. Courage is special because it is the natural expression of one of the other emotions. It is not a primary emotion of any Brain. The main reason

I want to spell this out is because courage is described in most books as the strong energy connected to the Gut Brain's fight response. You are probably familiar with the saying: "you need the guts to do it". I think that is a misunderstanding of how the Gut Brain works. The Gut Brain's anger or rage is thoughtless. It is not capable of self-sacrifice. The energy unleashed by Gut Brain rage is, in fact, focused entirely on self-preservation. So, as I see it, courage — true selfless courage — flows from the Heart Brain. If you consider courage to be a conscious decision to risk pain, peril or even death, to protect or preserve something more precious than one's own safety, there is no other place for courage to flow than from the Heart Brain.

Someone who is truly fearless is not capable of courage, since courage is to be found in the conscious over-riding of fear, not in being oblivious to it.

What then, ignites courage? Courage (as in standing up for your values and following what is good) comes from the emotion of love and the willingness to protect that love.

When you think about people who do incredible things to help other people, it is invariably rooted in compassion and love. Only love, real love, can override the survival mechanism of the Gut Brain. A parent who sacrifices his or her life to save a child, or people who donate a kidney for a family member, are the often unsung heroes of our world today.

In the movie Titanic, in which the character played by Leonardo DiCaprio sacrifices himself to save Kate Winslet, we see self-sacrifice rooted in love. If his Gut Brain was in charge, Leo would have shoved Kate into the dark, cold sea without a second thought.

Heart Brain stories are amazing in the movies. Love and compassion feel good. By watching these movies, we connect with those feelings and leave the movie theatre with a happy heart.

Just have a look at the top 5 movies all time

1. The Godfather (1972)
2. The Shawshank Redemption (1994)
3. Schindler's List (1993)
4. Raging Bull (1980)
5. Casablanca (1942)

All movies where the Heart is totally in charge, it is about family, friendship, bonding, courage, self-sacrificing.

I think it's fair to say that moral values are the territory of the Heart Brain. That is why people who have strong values are willing to die for them. Martin Luther King, or anyone willing to stand up to power, get their energy and commitment from their Heart Brain. For me at least, it makes me appreciate their courage even more when I think that even inside Martin Luther King or Gandhi, there was a Gut Brain screaming, "What are you doing? Shut up! Just take care of yourself!"

Another example is Nelson Mandela's willingness to follow his heart and reconcile with South Africa's white rulers, because he felt/thought it the best way to build a better, just nation or Rosa Parks who invigorated the struggle for racial equality when she refused to give up her bus seat to a white man in Montgomery, Alabama.

Why do we hate? And why is it healthy to do so?

All the positive Heart Brain emotions that we have been discussing have flip-sides. Despair, guilt, sadness, shame, aversion and hate also make their homes in our hearts. They, too, have a purpose. They are there to protect the heart; or help it heal when it has been injured.

Hate protects the Heart Brain from making the same mistake twice. It will protect us from trusting or connecting with that person a second time — just as the Gut Brain's disgust wards us away from foods that are toxic or rotten.

Hate is so powerful, though, that it can turn into violence. People can kill when they feel hate in their hearts, of course with some help from the Gut Brain.

Guilt and shame are great indicator emotions. They let us know when we have crossed the line in a relationship, for example, when we feel guilty because we did something that could hurt the connection or the other person, when we have breached our own values. We usually feel this because our Gut Brain took over for that moment and as a judge the Heart Brian evaluates the actions.

Guilt is also a strong emotion. If you do something that violates your own sense of right and wrong, you feel guilty. Making somebody else feel guilty so that they will do what we want them to is a well-known strategy (Gut Brain using the Heart Brain knowledge to get its way). There's even a term for it: 'guilt tripping'.

Guilt trips:

- If you love me, you would do that for me.
- Your father left me and now you're leaving me; everybody is leaving me.
- If you love me, you will eat this food.
- Go out with your friends and leave me alone.
- I carried you for nine months in the womb, took care of you and now you just disrespect me.

No matter what the relationship, guilt trips are a bad strategy. Every time we guilt trip our partner, we withdraw some money from our soulmate relationship.

Heart Brain domination: The love factor

Different people might make different choices in a situation they perceive as dangerous. Someone whose Heart Brain is dominant, that is, someone whose ingrained wiring is so profoundly oriented to collective, rather than individual survival might put themselves in the path of danger to protect the group. We hear about and admire such people. The parents who sacrifice themselves to save their child. The pilot who fights to keep the plane steady enough for the passengers to parachute safely. In virtually every case, you will find that it is love — the Heart Brain's ultimate trump card — that has the power to overcome the Gut Brain's compulsion to preserve 'the self' at all costs. What is really going on in cases like this is that the Heart Brain has redefined for the Gut Brain what 'the self' really is — to include loved ones, or even strangers.

Self-sacrifice can happen in small ways. Sometimes we take things like this for granted. When a parent works multiple jobs or goes to bed hungry, so their child is well cared for, that's Heart Brain love in action. It also happens in relationships. We often see one partner sacrificing personal rewards to support a loved one's success. (Admittedly, such things are not always clear-cut, as what benefits a couple in the long-term usually benefits both.)

EXAMPLE: DISCONNECTION

I still remember a couple who visited me.

She said, "I love my husband dearly. He is sweet, caring, always listens to me and gives me a cuddle when I need it (the Heart Brain connection is there), but I am not physically attracted anymore. He has gained 50 pounds in the last few years. After we make love, he turns around and falls asleep without considering my needs."

This is the Gut Brain complaint. When the Gut Brain is not happy with the appearance or sexual connection of the partner, finding those physical rewards elsewhere becomes a real danger to the relationship.

Tinder and Bumble are examples of the Gut Brain in action: Attractive? / Not Attractive? Gut Brains excel at binary black-and-white decisions. The text underneath the pictures is only rarely enough to create a Heart Brain or Head Brain connection. That part of the discussion commences after the initial Gut Brain match.

When you compare Tinder and Bumble, incidentally, you become aware right away that Bumble is aware of how most men make a Gut Brain decision. To increase the possibilities of a good match on Bumble, it is the woman who must send the first message. The thinking behind it is that a woman will decide based on the Heart Brain and Head Brain — but only when her Gut Brain feels safe.

9.

Head Brain Partners: logical, Rational, and as long it makes sense all is good

Having a relationship with a dominant Head Brain person is great as it is extremely safe, they will not cheat or betray and are there for you in their own way. And what is also a typical Head Brain situation? Just imagine you feel surprisingly enthusiastic after a day at work.

When you come home, you say to your Head Brain partner, "My boss asked me if I can work on a project, so I said yes. I think he really appreciates my efforts and good qualities; don't you think?"

Hoping for a positive response, instead you hear, "That doesn't make sense. You are already busy; you hardly have time for anything. You can't do this project; it is not logical for you to say yes to it. Maybe he is just clearing his own desk and filling yours".

When people are operating from the Head Brain, they will take an analytical approach to a regular situation, even when it is not needed (according to Heart or Gut Brain people). This can be risky, as the outcome will be a result of calculations on a presented set of parameters, and as we know, feelings and emotions are rather hard to put into an Excel spreadsheet. 'Believing' or 'trusting' are Heart and Gut Brain activities; the Head Brain does not trust or believe in good intentions, but uses historical data and comparisons to make the call.

With the best intentions, Head Brain people provide you with great alternatives that could be perceived as judgmental because they have not used empathy or have not read between the lines.

As you will understand when you read the section, Three Brain science, the theory is rooted in the work of Ivan Yakovlev. In his view, the development of the Head Brain was the result of the increasing complexity of human life. As we evolved from small bands of hunter-gatherer apes into small, then much larger, social groups, the most successful of our ancestors were the ones who could discern patterns in the world. This enabled them to make plans for the future, build things, make and use tools, express their ideas to others (language) and find creative ways to accomplish the tasks that needed to be done. Neither the Gut Brain, nor the Heart Brain, were up to that task, so a new intellectual engine evolved to enable the newly needed capabilities. So, the Head Brain evolved, not to supplant the Gut and Heart Brains, which were good at doing what they had always done, but to enhance them.

The Head Brain's purpose is to provide useful information to the Gut and Heart Brain. It might be a memory of how something is done, or a prediction of the future based on something it has learned. It does not get easily offended by the other Brains, since this Brain doesn't connect with them in terms of emotion. It remains logical and sometimes misses 'soft' clues. For social and emotional animals, this is a big missing piece, so the other Brains try to only let it loose when they need something from it. Head Brain advice must be worth a great deal, or humans would not have given it such a huge percentage of their body energy. Even so, Head Brains are hard to corral. When people "stay in their head", it means they do not go by the feelings of their Heart, but will be aware of the feelings of the Gut.

The Gut Brain commands the body to stay in the Head as a safe place, so as not to feel the Heart.

Phrases like,
"Why are you upset? There is nothing to be upset about,"
are therefore common from Head Brain mouths.
When they say,
"I don't understand",
this means they are missing emotional clues, and are doing their best to follow the emotions that they can identify.
Bear in mind that we all have a Gut Brain and sometimes this Brain is in charge in normal circumstances.

Mr. or Ms. Logical can turn every topic of conversation into a logical sequence. They think they can find a reasonable solution for everything in life and relationships. They can put everything on an Excel spreadsheet. Mr. or Ms. Logical is only focused on the facts, and misses out the important part where they were expected to complement their partner.

When a person is in their Head Brain, they forget the little white lie that makes the other person feel good, and instead emotionlessly state facts.

When you are on the scales and remark, "Hmm, I gained two pounds," you hope to get this kind of response: "It doesn't seem like it," or, "You still look amazing," but a Head Brain person may respond, "Yes! You are eating a lot these days; I knew it would go straight to your hips." Empathy, or even a compliment, would be a better response. But those sorts of things are not in the Head Brain's vocabulary.

Does the Head Brain Partner have emotions? Do logical emotions exist?

To the question, "Does the Head Brain Partner have emotions?" the answer is Yes and No. It has a driver that pushes us to learn, but it does not have the capacity to create or release hormones. The limbic brain has this, and we don't feel them in our Head, the Limbic Brains actions are solely there to activate the body.

What the Head Brain does have is:

- Curiosity
- Interest
- Surprise
- Disagreement
- Judgement

Our Head Brain has a thirst for learning and knowledge, like a dry sponge being placed in a bucket of water. This results in the traits of curiosity, interest, and surprise.

On the other hand, when it thinks something is true, it's stubborn and disregards new information. It distorts or deletes whatever new information arrives that does not fit the current fixed ideas. There are moments when the Head Brain can take over the Heart Brain or Gut Brain, just think about those movies where, although the person sees the chainsaw, they are still curious enough to enter the room. Therefore, these are not real emotions, more drivers.

To be clear, the Head Brain, or logical brain, is not an empathy brain, and this lack of emotion from the Head Brain is easy to explain.

When we want to make decisions objectively and consistently, turning off the emotional system is essential. When we let feelings interfere with our decisions, the spur of the moment could change the decision and, therefore, the outcome as well.

For example, I don't know how many times this has happened to you; I know it happens to me. I am angry because something has happened, then a minute later my mother is on the phone and I am snappy with her. Research has shown that when anger is triggered in one situation, it automatically elicits a motive to blame individuals in other situations, even though the targets of such anger have nothing to do with the source of the anger.[36]

And just imagine that a dentist who is doing some work on you gets emotional and shares: "I cannot do it as it will hurt you" and starts crying or almost worse gets angry when it does not work the first time and fueled with anger starts drilling and filing your tooth. In those moments you are extremely happy that the Head Brain dominated dentist is not being ruled by emotions.

Once I was working with a couple who had little interaction with each other. I realized that they were communicating from different starting points, and from their different Brains. I asked her, "What would you really like to have more of in this relationship?" She replied, while looking at her partner, "I would love to spend more time together," (as in being together — Heart Brain wish).

After her partner heard her say this, he looked surprised and, nodding his head, replied, "I only went out once last week. The rest of the week I was at home all the time." Yes, based on real data and facts, the husband was right, but that was not what she meant. Being in the same house is not always time together, at least not from her point of view.

They were both talking from a different Brain. Both lacked the capacity to connect with the other person's Brain. Even though they were both right, they did not understand each other.

Do either of the following conversations ring a bell?

You: Oh damn! I spilled something over my dress.

Response: Yes, you should have used a napkin, or Yes, that will leave a bad stain.

You: What do you think, the red or the blue shirt?

Response: Both are okay.

Both examples are where the Head Brain is in charge for the response, in other words, the logical brain is in charge.

If you are looking for an example of the ultimate Head Brain person, just watch Star Trek. Spock, the half-human/half-alien First Officer, is an emotionless creature whose mind is ruled only by logic. Sheldon, from the series The Big Bang, is another such creature.

Just to be clear, before our discussion of Head Brain-dominant people starts to make their thinking process seem like popular notions of autism, that is not the case. Autism is a much more complex system of interactions in the Head Brain that is far beyond the scope of this book. Autism is something that involves much more — and is far more complicated — than having difficulty processing emotions or reading social cues. In addition, autistic people can have amazing hearts and can really care about someone else.

In the head, we have a huge store of experiences, facts (both observed and acquired), and theories and predictions about the future. The Head Brain's job is to use that knowledge to provide creative and insightful ways to solve problems. When neither of them is derailed by trauma or bad information, the Gut Brain and the Head Brain work well together.

This is especially true for the part of the Gut Brain focused on self-preservation. In the Section, The science behind our Three Brains, we will go into some depth about the research work between the Gut Brain and Head Brain, done by the Russian-born neuropathologist, Ivan Yakovlev. Yakovlev's studies have led him to conclude that, after the Heart Brain evolved to meet the mammalian need for connection and community, the Head Brain evolved to assist the Gut Brain's decision-making.[37]

The best example of how the Head Brain does its best to serve the Gut or Heart Brains, but is not in charge, is anxiety and depression.

When you are anxious about something, it is because you anticipate some fear becoming real. Anxiety flows, therefore, from the Gut Brain. The Gut Brain then will ask the Head Brain to provide a solution. When the Gut Brain hears back that the Head Brain has devised a solution that is 100% guaranteed to lead to a safe outcome, the Gut Brain will relax.

There you go. Problem solved. But what if your Head Brain can't absolutely guarantee that the solution will work? Head Brains can deal with uncertainty. Gut Brains want security. So, the Gut Brain stays anxious, which stimulates the Head Brain to keep on thinking. Faced with such impossible demands, the Head Brain ties itself in knots to try to calm down the Gut Brain. When it can't succeed, the Gut Brain goes to its last-resort state of immobilization. The result of all of this is depression — a state of biological hopelessness.

Example: When the Head Brain is right

On YouTube, you can find a video called It's not about the nail.[38] *It shows in a perfect way how the Head Brain deals with an issue, with the objective to solve it.*

In this video, a woman is talking about the pressure she feels inside her head, an aching pressure in her head and her fear that it will never stop.

The response she receives from her boyfriend upon sharing this information is, "Yeah, you know you have a nail in your head". (The funny thing in the video is that she does have a nail in her head, so factually, he is right.)

She responds to this in a way that shows that she likes to be heard instead of being presented with a solution. In a sharp voice she says, "It is not about the nail!"

As the boyfriend thinks he is right, he gives it another try, like Head Brain people love to do, because the other person did not really understand the first time. He goes on, "Are you sure? Because I bet if we get that nail out, it's over."

And then it happens, the crack in the miscommunication becomes extremely obvious.

She screams in a loud voice, also with strong non-verbal communication, "STOP trying to fix it!"

In the case of a real Head Brain person, when they think that they are right, they will not give up easily. Maintaining this behavior, her boyfriend once again says, "I'm not trying to fix it, I'm just pointing out that there is physically a nail in your head".

Now you see after four times trying to do his best to be understood, and hearing her verbal slap (the Head Brain asked for help from the Gut Brain and as we read in a previous chapter, the Gut Brain prepared to attack in response to this), she says: "You are always doing it, you are always trying to fix things, while I would just like you to listen."

Can you see him being totally thrown out of the field and deciding to change the route to save the day? This is extremely hard for a Head Brain to do. We need to develop Heart Brain to make this detour.

He says, "I'm listening," puts on an emphatic face, tilts his head a little bit and starts listening while she continues to tell her story.

She explains how her headache causes her sleeping issues, and that her shirts get torn up when she takes them off.

Then he responds beautifully from the heart, "That sounds really hard."

Just a note: in real life it could also be that this is a learned response, like a Pavlov dog conditioned to respond. Like when you hear a question from your partner about which outfit is better, your response is without even thinking, "They both look amazing on you."

Now when she finally feels like she is listened to and he finally understands how she feels, she responds beautifully, "It really is. Thank you," and wants to give him a kiss as a thank you for rebuilding the connection between them.[39] In the last scene of the video, as they try to kiss, the nail gets in the way. The Head Brain of the guy once again compels him to provide a solution, and the girl again shouts, "STOP!'

Although this video/conversation is quite funny and ironic because there is a nail in her head, so on a factual basis he is right, it also explains the difficulty in building up a connection between a Head Brain-dominant person and a Heart Brain-dominant person. The first response is what the average Head Brain person does, it is logical, more focused on the solution, period.

How does the Head Brain express thoughts as "emotions"?

When we have a disturbed connection between Head and Heart/Gut, the Head Brain person rationalizes their feelings. It can become a bit messy; the Head does not know what the emotions are that are being sent, or the line between Head and Heart/Gut is unclear.

That means that facts (Head logic) are connected to feelings and therefore they are not really emotions at all.

EXAMPLE: HEAD BRAIN INTERPRETATION OF HEART AND GUT BRAINS' FEELINGS

I remember a couple that had such an issue. Their communication went like this:

He said, "I feel inadequate as your partner, because it feels unreasonable for me to do the things you expect from me."

She responded, "You don't have to feel inadequate. It's just that I don't feel understood when you don't listen to me."

Here the Head Brain is making sense of what the Heart Brain or Gut Brain are feeling.

Words like 'inadequate', 'unreasonable' and 'understood' are not expressions of emotion. Just think about it, how do you feel and where do you feel it when you feel inadequate? You actually feel frustrated, angry, or disappointed — these are emotions.

His Head Brain made an assessment or judgment on his ability as a partner, based on a feeling he had in the Heart or Gut Brains.

I asked him not to analyze it, but to put his hands on his stomach and feel how it felt there when he was saying: "Because it feels unreasonable for me to do the things you expect from me." I asked him to say it as many times as it took for him to start to feel something in his Gut Brain (like the exercise in Chapter 2).

He said after some time, "My gut feels tense and is squeezing together. It feels like fear."

Then he continued, "I feel fearful in myself as a partner for you, because I cannot fulfill your needs. Or maybe it is better to say I feel frustrated with myself as a partner for you because I cannot fulfill your needs."

Her eyes welled up when she heard that. I asked her to put her hands on her heart and really communicate from there. She said, "I feel lonely when you don't look at me when I talk to you and when I don't receive acknowledgement from you, to show that you have heard what I said."

In his book Nonviolent Communication, Marshall Rosenberg provides a great list of surrogate feelings used by the Head Brain to do its best to express actual feelings:

Abandoned, abused, attacked, betrayed, bullied, cheated, diminished, distrusted, interrupted, intimidated, let down, manipulated, misunderstood, neglected, overworked, patronized, pressured, provoked, put down, rejected, taken for granted, threatened, unappreciated, unheard, unseen, unsupported, unwanted and used.[40]

One solution to feeling what kind of emotions they express is to carry out the exercise in the later in this book (Chapter 10: "How do your Brains talk to you?"), which I use with my clients.

Whether communication between the Three Brains will happen or not depends on how well you can express feelings coming from the Gut, and/or from the Heart and how well you can distinguish them from rational observations or judgments.

When the Head Brain is doing its best to lead, it could make the situation more complex than necessary.

This is explained by David Dotlich in his book Head, Heart and Guts: How the World's Best Companies Develop Complete Leaders.[41]

"People who lead only from the Head run the risk of overthinking problems and overanalyzing opportunities.

Rather than outlining options clearly or providing just enough data to make a decision, they believe any problem is a set of intellectual challenges, and consequently they overwhelm everyone with statistics, ideas, and alternatives.

They may lack the guts to confront the emotional dynamics of the situation or delay in deciding.

Their complex approach causes people to question their own simpler (and often more effective) ideas, and they defer to complexity."

Head Brain domination: Let's puzzle this out

Some people are dominated by their Head Brains. Test pilots and surgeons are extreme examples of people who are trained to treat even life-or-death situations simply as intellectual problems. They keep their Gut Brains silent, having trained it that the only real path to safety is the logic and knowledge of their Head Brains.

As you will read in the section, The science behind our Three Brains, and the discoveries of Ivan Yakovlev, the Head Brain's complexity and awesome powers are used as an advisor.

Yes, you read that correctly: the Head Brain is completely devoted to its task of feeding the Gut and Heart Brains with predictions for the future, based on its experiences and the things that it has been told or read. Like any good counsellor, Head Brains are not easily offended. This Brain doesn't connect with the other Brains (or with itself) on emotional terms at all. It is a purely logical machine — an internal Mr Spock. Like Star Trek's Spock, Head Brains often miss social cues. The other Brains know this, of course, and they only let it socialize when they feel that it is safe (Gut Brain) and not socially awkward (Heart Brain).

One reason people sometimes 'stay' in their Head Brains in times of emotional turmoil, is that the Gut Brain is trying to minimize emotional damage by walling off the Heart Brain's powerful feelings. In almost every trauma experience, we disassociate from the bodily experiences, as a protection mechanism, as you can read in the section, The science behind our Three Brains; this is when the dorsal vagal nerve gets activated — the immobilization nerve. Usually, we return to normal rather quickly. Only when the trauma is overwhelming (and for every person that threshold is different), the Gut Brain can decide to stay in that mode and let us only operate from the Head Brain.

Sentences like,
"Why are you upset, there is nothing to be upset about,"
are therefore common from these people's mouths.
If, in a moment of high emotion, someone says,
"I don't understand why you feel that way,"
that tells you they have put the wrong Brain into gear — and
failed to grasp the emotional cues.

So how do you apply this information? Become aware of your partner's (or friend or anyone you are interacting with) default state. Are they a Head Brain person or a Heart Brain person? And always be aware that if something feels unsafe, the Gut Brain will take control, no matter who is usually running the show. The same goes for times in which the person is hungry, thirsty, or is completely swayed by sexual lust or desire. In those cases, the power and aggression of their actions may startle or even alarm you.

Just as it feels normal when our Brains are aligned, disagreements amongst our Brains are natural and inevitable. In fact, our Brains work best when they disagree and resolve those disagreements. Problems arise, not from the disagreement itself, but from what is creating the disagreement and how it is resolved. As we discussed earlier, our Three Brains make decisions differently and by evaluating different things.

So, when you are faced with some decision that looks different from different angles, each of your Brains will have its own opinion about what decision you should make — or at least what criteria need to be considered.

To understand how the same experience can teach different lessons to our different Brains, consider the following illustration.

EXAMPLE: HOW OUR DIFFERENT BRAINS CAN SEE THE SAME THING IN DIFFERENT WAYS

I once worked with a group of siblings whose parents were divorced. When I met them as young adults, I discovered that each one had a totally different view on how their parents had raised them.

The oldest son had sympathy and empathy for his dad. He saw him as a good-hearted person who was not strong enough to deal with his mother. He perceived his mother as an egotist who loved to portray herself as a victim.

This young man told me he was longing for love and a profound connection based on trust and support. He was afraid to commit. You never know, he told me, if a lovely woman would turn out like my mother did. This young man's Gut Brain was protecting his Heart Brain. His Heart Brain was really seeking for connection and trust, but his Gut Brain associated those things with pain and would not let his heart make a successful connection.

The second child, a daughter, declared that her parents should never have been together in the first place. Dad was born and raised in Australia. Mom was from Germany. It was their different cultural backgrounds, she thought, that had doomed her parents' marriage. Now, the daughter wanted to return to Europe — and was in a relationship with a young German. Although her Heart Brain believed in real love and connection, her Head Brain had concluded that, like her mother, she could never find happiness with an Australian like her dad.

The youngest son believed that his father was weak, and that he had failed to deliver in his role as a father. He thought his mother was totally right to demand that her husband change his behavior — and that, if he could not, then it was best that he leaves.

This young man was pursuing a career and was living a Gut Brain-dominated male role. He believed that a man had to be the bread-winner of the family and a woman's role was to support her man. He and his wife had a child, he was working and she was at stay-at-home mom, taking care of the child, cooking, cleaning, and supporting the household. He said he deliberately went for a partner who was, as he put it, not as educated as he was and would not be a threat to his authority. He said he did not really believe in real love and that every relationship is a trade-off, doing the best for the system. We could say his partner and he were living a life based on a Gut Brain and Head Brain connection.

10.

Is it love or sex with your Three Brains?

Everybody in an intimate relationship has intimate moments in the bedroom. Through all my studies and research, I have realized that making love is where the last layer of safety, trust, rejection and honesty is tested. One of the reasons this subject is so hard is that for some reason it is taboo to talk about sex. A child of 12 can watch television and see how people kill each other, but they need to be 18 to watch people making love or having sex. Most parents do not do an amazing job in educating their kids on sex or making love, and in schools it is often also taboo.

Another reason it is a difficult area is that sex is a very intimate and vulnerable action between the two of you; to make it beautiful, your two Heart Brains must be open and connected, and your Gut Brains need to feel safe. As most couples are not used to talking about sex, and are only slightly educated in what to do and not do, and in what is 'normal' and 'abnormal', the fear of rejection when you're sharing your own preferences or dislikes is strong. So, most people do not share in the bedroom what they like or do not like and hope that the other knows without having to tell them.

A colleague of mine, a relationship/sex counsellor, says that in more than 90% of couples' therapy, talking about sex makes her clients blush. As she says, if you cannot feel safe there, it is tainting the relationship for sure sooner or later.

How is it for you? Do you really dare to share your likes and dislikes in the bedroom, and do you know what you partner likes or does not like?

The moment the answer is not 100% yes, you can be sure your Three Brains disagree about having their needs/wishes fulfilled in the bedroom.

One part of the Gut Brain is begging, "Please talk about what I like and don't like," but the Heart Brain is many times afraid for being rejected if it expresses their own needs.

Only when there is true trust the Heart Brain could, based, on the connection there is with the other person, dare to open up for its own needs.

The Head Brain does its best to figure out how it should communicate this, because "it was never taught to me; where do I find the information to learn all of this?"

We need all Three Brains to have the ultimate love-making experience.

How about testing the extent of your Head Brain's knowledge:

What is the difference for you between making love and sex?

How much do you know about the importance of kissing, giving attention, different positions, how oral or anal sex works, and, more importantly, how you can do these so that they are pleasurable for both partners? Are you aware of the love strategies that we could have? The stages we have in relationships?

And, an extra test question, did you know that women can experience at least three different types of orgasms?

I wonder what you thought when you read the last question? Is one or more of your Brains sending out signals of interest, or shame, or maybe incompetence etc.? Depending on what you felt, it could signal a misaligned Brain.

And is it not strange that we may blush or have strong emotions reading this, but easily watch the latest movie where people shoot and kill each other?

How do our Three Brains address sex or lovemaking differently?

It's important to address this, as lust and desire are primary emotions from the Gut Brain.

To be clear, sex is the domain of the Gut Brain, and making love is the domain of the Heart Brain. The Head Brain is not needed during sex or lovemaking, it is more of a hindrance. The Head Brain is needed beforehand, to get equipped with the knowledge.

Furthermore, as human beings, we have three different sexual/sensual desires: sex, making love, or both at the same time.

It is not the purpose of this book to go into detail of how to have amazing sex or lovemaking, more how our Three Brains perceive it and support it, how they are connected with our pleasure organs and what their needs are (if you would like to read more about technique, I could recommend David Deida's book, The Enlightened Sex Manual).

At this point, I would like to emphasize the importance of feeling safe to express your needs and wishes in the bedroom.

One of the golden rules of having a satisfying sex life is being able to express these needs and wishes freely and safely, without the fear of being judged or rejected. This does not mean your partner has to accept all your wishes and needs and carry them out, it is much more that you both are able to express them and find common ground in how you can connect with each other.

Gut Brain means sex

Gut Brain sex follows the primal desires of reproduction.

I call it 'friction-based sex'. This is the sex you can see in most porn movies — different positions are all based on friction, giving the desired end result.

I don't mean to give the impression this is not good sex. Not at all, there is absolutely nothing wrong with this kind of sex, it is based on our primary lust instincts, so it has a valid reason to be there. Lovemaking takes more time, so this more primal sex is good, for example, when you do not have a lot of time. There is nothing wrong with energized Gut Brain sex in the bedroom, kitchen, on the couch or somewhere outside.

However, when couples only have this Gut Brain sex, they risk wearing out the connection. Often, when we are not happy with our sex life, this is the only sex there is. It usually leads to unfulfilled desires; it could mean we do not have an orgasm and only our partner does before falling asleep (egoistic Gut Brain sex), or that we have an unfulfilled Heart Brain need for connection/lovemaking.

In both cases, communication is needed.

Gut and Heart Brain is sex/lovemaking

When we talk about Heart Brain sex, we are actually talking about lovemaking. In lovemaking, it's not only about the sex but also about the connection before and after the Gut Brain fun. This means feeling loved, appreciated, and that our partner likes to take care of our needs and we like to take care of their needs.

This could mean having that nice dinner, connecting in some way (cuddling, talking etc.) and after the sex is finished, the lovemaking goes on.

It requires not only bedroom techniques, but feeling a connection with each other, physically and emotionally. It means opening up to your own needs/wishes and to those of the other person. Both require a connection with their own Heart and with the Heart of their partner.

It also means not thinking of your own pleasure first, but thinking instead, "How can I please the other, not just myself?"

EXAMPLE: WHAT HAPPENS IF WE DO NOT FEEL SAFE? A GUT BRAIN WOMAN AND HER PARTNERS

One of my previous clients was a strong, self-confident woman, who spoke out about what she wanted and didn't want, daring to take the fight if people disagreed. She said that when she was going out with men, and reached the intimate part of the relationship, a lot of men could not perform because of her self-confidence and strength of character (Gut Brain).

Men tend to be socialized to have a developed Gut Brain, to be dominant; the provider. So, when a Gut Brain man becomes aware that his partner also has a strong Gut Brain, and dares to challenge his own, his Gut Brain could feel attacked and become afraid. When this happens, the 'normal' response is silence, escaping, withdrawing, or playing dead. Actions you really don't like to happen in the bedroom, neither for him, nor for her. It should be fun in the bedroom, not another battle of the sexes.

So, when we talked it through, it became clear that the men who could perform more successfully were those who were well connected to their Heart Brain, and had high self-esteem, not a fear of being rejected. They felt that sex or performing was not the only part that made them who they were but thought of it as lovemaking and that learning how to do that with a new partner means sometimes doing the 'wrong' thing.

Section 4.

HOW TO DEAL WITH THE HEAD, HEART OR GUT BRAIN PARTNERS? THE KEY: WHICH BRAIN IS TALKING?

11.

How do your Brains talk to you?

Now we covered all the characteristics of the Three Brains and you have an insight into what your dominance is and probably also have an insight into how that is for the people around you lets go to: what to do with all of that? How do we connect better, communicate better etc.?

First things first, how do your Three Brains communicate with you?

Exercise: Listening to your own Three Brains language

As the saying goes, "the proof of the pudding is in the eating". The following short exercise will let you experience how your Three Brains communicate with you (the sensations you become aware of) and make decisions. This activity is designed to reveal how your Brains react to things that are perceived TRUE and things that are perceived FALSE.

Step 1: Connecting with your HEAD Brain

- Place both of your feet flat on the floor.
- Take a deep breath in, then exhale gently, without forcing out the air.
- Repeat this a couple of times until you feel more relaxed.

- Now place your index and middle finger on your forehead just above the middle of your eyebrows.
- Say out loud (really say it out loud because all the nerve systems will then be activated, whereas if you only think the words, not all the nerve systems are activated): "My name is ...." (Use your own first name).

Notice how your Head responds.

Somewhere you can become aware of a notion of, "Yes, that is true".

Step 2: Connecting with your HEART Brain:

- Place the same two fingers on your heart.
- Take a deep breath in, then exhale gently, without forcing out the air, and relax.
- Say out loud: "My name is ...." (Use the same name).

Notice how your Heart responds.

It could be that your Heart responds differently than your Head, no words but more sensations around the heart area, warmth, a smile etc. Even so, it could feel true to you.

Step 3: Connecting with your GUT Brain

- Place the same two fingers on your abdomen, just below your navel.
- Take a deep breath in, then exhale gently, without forcing out the air, and relax.
- Say out loud: "My name is ...." (Use the same name).

Notice how your Gut responds.

It is possible, though not certain, that your Gut Brain will respond differently than your Head or Heart with maybe different sensations.

This exercise is designed to show how you react when you hear something you know to be true on all three Brain levels, although we learned that truth at different ages and with different memories and emotions and therefore could notice a variety of responses to the same truth. Our name, which is the truest thing about our personality, is great for this exercise.

Step 4: How do your Three Brains react to something FALSE?

- Pick any name you want — anything that is **not** your real name.
- Now, repeat the above exercise using the name that is not yours.

Notice how your Brains respond very differently to something they know to be untrue.

This exercise shows the (emotional) effect that words have on your Three Brains and the way they remember and relate words to memories and emotions to make decisions and how they communicate that back.

If you would like to experience how emotional memories have a more profound effect on your Three Brains, repeat the same exercise using your nickname or something you are called by the people near and dear to you.

You will certainly get a different emotional response to that name from your Heart Brain and your Gut Brain, than when you carried out the first exercise.

12.

How to find out: which Brain is talking? The language and words of our Three Brains

Did you ever have that experience where you felt that your emotions were taking over and the words you were saying were directed from those emotions? How do we know that actually that is not always the case and that our 'hidden' emotions are in control? How do we know that what we say is actually a true expression of our intention and in such a way that the other person really grasps what we are saying?

There is a way that is both easy and difficult at the same time: when you have a conversation and are observing whilst also listening to the words as they will share traces of which of their Three Brains are talking.

Knowing which words are typical words of the Three Brains will help avert the connection disasters that can ensue when you connect to the wrong Brain, or trigger it with an unfortunate choice of words.

Let's look at an example to understand why it is so important to choose the right words? For instance, your partner asks you to go to a movie you dislike.

The fist important thing to know about Communication: we can't not respond.

So, just imagine if you stay silent (Gut Brain in control with an avoiding tactic) and pretend you didn't hear them. Do you respond or not?

Actually yes, even when you stay silent, you are responding.

Your partner could interpret your behavior as you not paying attention to them (their Heart Brain has that 6th sense for feeling rejection) that we don't listen, that will take the next 30 minutes to fix their feelings. Or they ask for our attention and ask it again.

So, pitifully, there is no easy way out for you, you always have to respond.

When you would like to say no, it is wise to be careful how you are saying no to going to the movie while also saying yes to your partner.

In this case, if you say a blunt "no", you could have to explain exactly why you don't like the movie, their head wants to understand the reason. Their heart would like to know if you are saying no to them, and their gut is curious what else you would like to do instead of pleasing them? Yes, it is a mine field.

If you say yes, you could spoil your own evening.

In all cases, you did respond and probably will have a discussion between your own Heart Brain that says to be nice to your partner and go to the movies. Whereas your Gut Brain wants to take care of you, the boss, and compels you not to go.

Before we play out the scenario, let's look at some frequently used trigger words, positive and negative.

Gut Brain words

Soothing

- all right
- calm
- comfortable
- fulfilled
- safe
- satisfied

Alarming

- contempt
- dangerous/afraid
- disgust
- furious
- hungry/thirsty
- pain
- scary
- wrong

Heart Brain words

Connecting

- connection
- family
- good
- love
- sorry
- us/we

Disconnecting

- disconnected
- guild
- hate
- lonely
- unfriendly
- not nice

Head Brain words

Confirming

- logical
- makes sense
- true
- right
- think
- remember
- tomorrow/future

Judging

- doesn't make sense
- illogical
- stupid
- strange
- wrong
- not true

As a rule of thumb to gain an insight into which Brain is active from your partner when they are talking, it is actually rather easy:

Head Brain language is always logical, fact based, is about cause and effect. This as the head has the objective to understand and predict.

Examples:

- It's the intelligent thing to do
- It makes sense
- Let's discuss this like adults
- Let's evaluate the pros and cons
- Let's make it concrete
- Off the top of my head
- One's eyes are popping out of one's head
- Over one's head
- Rear its ugly head (a problem or something unpleasant)

Heart Brain language on the other hand is recognizable as it is always about, connection, others, feelings based on values, right and wrong.

Examples:

- Capture, steal or win one's heart (make someone fall in love)
- Close, dear or near to one's heart (loved or valued by someone)
- Cross one's heart (an oath to assert one's honesty)
- Didn't have the heart (when one can't summon the will to do something)
- Eat your heart out (mocking someone, expressing the desire for suffering; usually facetious)
- Faint of heart (lacking courage)
- Find it in one's heart (have the compassion or courage)

Gut Brain language can be identified as it is action and/or oriented, about what it means for you, and everything that is connected with the digestive system.

Examples:

- Hard to swallow
- Hate one's guts

- I feel sick in my stomach
- I have a stone in my stomach
- Kick in the guts
- This smells like….
- I don't have the guts to achieve my dreams.

I know there are many more words; the idea is not to make a comprehensive list, but more to guide what kind of words are 'positive' for each Brain, and which ones are more 'negative' and how you can identify them

SCENARIO — THE MOVIE COMPROMISE

Your partner asks you to go to a movie that your Gut Brain is pretty sure you will hate. "Yuck! I'm gonna hate that movie!" it says. Don't ever expect any subtlety or an extended vocabulary from your (or anyone else's) Gut Brain. And remember, saying nothing is also a common Gut Brain response — Gut Brains love it when a problem just goes away.

Letting your Gut Brain run the show here is likely to lead to a conflict. Being no fool, you consult your Heart Brain.

Most likely, your Heart Brain leans toward nurturing togetherness, sucking it up and going to the movie. Depending on the value you place on the relationship, that might end the discussion right there. The Heart would remind the Gut that offending your partner is not a safe thing to do and off you would both go to the multiplex.

One other option might keep your partner and your Three Brains happy — add your Head Brain to the discussion. Maybe it can propose something that keeps everyone happy — even your RomCom-hating Gut Brain. After all, this evening is one among many. There is the future to consider. And the future is the Head

Brain's area of expertise. Your Head Brain might propose something inventive like, "Let's do the movie tonight, but tomorrow let's go to the beach."

Now comes the time for some internal discussion. Your Heart Brain reports to your Gut Brain that, with a little patience, it will be rewarded with a beach day. The Gut Brain will be likely to agree to postpone its gratification.

Three Brains word disasters

Another rule of learning 'how to fit with your partner' is even trickier. One minor detail can mean the difference between having a warm interaction or a conflict.

We can all think of a time when we had a great chat with somebody, then just one little thing flipped the entire situation 180 degrees.

It may go like this: Your partner asks, "How do I look?" or "Do you like my outfit?" If you are busy with something else, none of your Brains are probably aware of the intention of your partner's question: honest feedback or a compliment?

Your Gut Brain is not truly interested as there is no personal gain.

Your Head Brain looks only at the data. If you let either of them answer without checking the intention behind the question, you may find yourself in trouble.

If you don't have time to check the intention, then such questions are the rightful domain of the Heart Brain's focus on amity and serenity.

The Heart Brain's answer, "You look terrific!" is then the only correct response.

In other words, if you need to reply without connecting/thinking, let your Heart Brain respond if you want to have a nice evening.

In a situation like this, every time we offer a critique (a Gut Brain or Head Brain response), we miss the point of exchanges like this — to strengthen the bonds of attachment and affection.

Now, imagine you're having dinner with a loved one or a friend. Out of the blue, your partner or friend says: "If I were you, I would not eat so much."

What is your first thought? It sounds like a criticism. Criticisms make the target feel threatened. Threats are the Gut Brain's department and it fires up.

Do they think I'm fat? Is my eating causing offence or disgust? (The Gut Brain senses danger and reacts.)

Your dinner partner could be trying to tell you to save room for a delicious dessert. But that clarification might come too late. One ill-considered remark likely ruined the entire experience.

Juggling the impulses of three very different perspectives can be dangerous for someone who is impulsive. Training yourself to wait for one second to become aware of which Brain is offering its opinion (and then refusing to give voice to the personally insensitive ones) can avert many bruised friendships.

13.

Partnership: What are the Two magic bullets?

So now the time has come to start applying what we have learnt to the important relationships in our lives. For most of us, that is our relationship with our partners/caregivers, kids, family, friends, and colleagues.

What do you do if you are listening to a radio station and the reception is terrible? You adjust the tuning. The most important thing to understand about applying our three-Brain insights to our interactions with other people is that each of them has Three Brains too. And how they interact with one another, and with us, is going to be a result of how each of those Brains experienced life before we met them. It is always a challenge to figure out what is going on in someone else's mind — and our insights have only made it clearer how complicated it can be.

As we know by now, the Brain we usually talk to in another person, the Head Brain, is only rarely the root of whatever problem we are trying to address. For that, we need to be aware of (and sometimes get into contact with) their Heart Brain and Gut Brain. They are the real powers behind the Head Brain's throne, and they have their own agendas. And everyone's mix of experiences and traumas is different. So, naturally enough, our Brains are aligned in ways very different from our partner's. No wonder couples have difficulties fitting together!

Just think about your parents, partner or a good friend. What do you experience when you think about them? What do you feel in your Head? In your Heart? In your Gut? Take the most used three-word sentence in the world: "I love you." Imagine your mother, partner and friend saying this to you in a sweet voice. Now imagine them saying it in a loud, snappy voice. The same sentence can have more than 20 different meanings, making you experience an even greater number of reactions in your Head, Heart or Gut.

AT THE BEACH: ADULTS, CHILDREN AND TEENS

While I'm writing this, I'm in a café close to the beach in Perth, Australia.

I see little children playing in the sand and with shells. They are laughing, running, screaming, and jumping into the sea. To my eyes, I am seeing balanced Brains at play. The parents and other adults are mostly sitting there, looking at their smartphones. Among the adults, I don't see many happy, smiling faces — or even people who look as though they are enjoying themselves. It is as if smiling and happiness disappears when we become adults.

The adults seem to be disconnected from their surroundings — and even from their lives. They seem tired and stressed. If so, their Gut Brains are in command and the Gut Brain is all about "me" — it takes over when we're worried, or life seems too complicated. Gut Brains are excellent simplifiers.

But why would people want to disconnect from their lives? I propose that their fatigue is rooted in inner conflict. Their Brains are not aligned — and even the simplest decision seems overwhelming.

So how can we connect with our Brains and their needs? What are the magic bullets?

Magic bullet 1:

In the realm of human relations, the simplest rule will be this: **Your Heart Brain will be your best guide— if it lets the Gut Brain keep it safe and it lets the Head Brain keep it wise.** The French writer, Antoine de Saint-Exupéry, expressed that wisdom more poetically in The Little Prince:

"Goodbye," said the fox. "And now here is my secret, a very simple secret: It is only with the heart that one can see rightly; what is essential is invisible to the eye." "What is essential is invisible to the eye," the Little Prince repeated, so that he would be sure to remember. "Men have forgotten this truth," said the fox.

Golden rule

When we would really like to understand somebody else, we must listen with our Heart Brain and utilize our Head Brain to make sense of what is being said. We can then become aware of our partner's internal processes. In that case we can become aware: "which brain is talking?"

To truly engage in this behavior we have to silence our own little critical voice in our Head Brain and the advice of our Gut Brain that tries its best not to engage if their is no personal gain. When these two Brains are active, our listening skills and communication skills can deteriorate.

That does not mean we should not listen to our Head or Gut Brains, but observe them first to see if they are giving valid warnings, or are merely producing a response based on our previous experiences.

Now that you know the most important rule — see with the Heart — and how the Three Brains react to different situations, you are ready to put that knowledge to use. Make no mistake, your Three Brains can work together to control how you connect to other people and determine what the emotional quality of that connection will be. You can choose (or at least strongly influence) which of your Brains is doing the connecting, and which of theirs you connect to.

As we have learned, the first piece of the puzzle to understanding your partner, colleague, boss, parent or kid is to understand yourself. We learned in earlier chapters how to align our own Brains. Now it's time to open them to make a connection with someone else.

Magic bullet 2:

Before you do that and look with the Heart, there is a second rule you need to check: **"Do I feel personally safe?" If not, STOP**. Even though I truly believe in the goodness of people there are still many messed up people who are dominated by their selfish Gut Brain. Trying to save or please them could cause us personal harm or failure and disappointments. There are too many examples of people who stayed with their partner and ended up in a bad way or worked their butt off for their boss and ended up with a burnout.

You cannot connect with anyone until your Gut Brain has dropped its guard, as you are sure you're safe, and is ready to let the Heart and the Head do their magic of feeling and thinking.

14.

How to engage with the Head, Heart and Gut Brain, the eighteen golden rules

So, now, once you feel safe, how do you establish a connection?

The Rules are there to create Three Brains Aligned communication. Just talking to one of them will never give the full answer.

Just imagine you are really hungry and you are standing in front of your fridge, you have the door open and you see the healthy section with veggies, the savory section with cakes and the left-over section of pizza and I ask you "what would you really like to eat" or I would ask you "what would be wise to eat now?"

For most of us we have 2 different answers as the 2 questions activate two different Brains and what they prefer.

So, with the rules we create an environment that we can connect with that brain to get the insights.

In order to do so, let's go through all eighteen rules of engagement to deal with the different types of Brains:

8 rules for dealing with Gut Brains: take it safe

Four rules for dealing with Head Brains: understand before being understood

six rules for dealing with Heart Brains: stay connected

Yes, the Head only 4 and the Gut 8. Connecting with Head Brain people is "easy" however the Gut Brain is a bit more complex and it is not the most social one to say the least.

The 8 rules of dealing with Gut Brain dominated people

Rule 1: Assess where the other person is. Do they feel safe?

Even when everything is safe it does not mean they feel safe. If they don't, is there something you can do or say that will help their Gut Brain open the door to a connection? Only when their Gut Brain feels safe and satisfied, it relaxes. When it does, it opens the door to their Heart and Head Brains. But when their Gut Brain is alarmed, there is no 'Us' but only 'Me'. It does not matter what gender you are, the instant we feel unsafe, our Gut Brain takes control. Communication and actions will be entirely focused on getting back to safety, meaning getting control or power over the situation.

Their Gut Brain, of course, might be fired up for its own reasons. If it is, and you can't soothe it (most likely because the danger it perceives has nothing to do with you), then STOP! Until they feel safe, there is nothing to connect to. Their self-protective Gut Brain will keep that door closed.

It is important to understand here that it's very difficult to connect to someone's Gut Brain directly. Gut Brains don't really listen to outsiders. But do observe them. The only way to truly set someone's Gut Brain at ease is for it to experience that it is safe. This can take time. And it is subtle. Anything that looks or feels like aggression or impatience will set off the Gut Brain's alarms and it will shut you out.

This makes connecting with Gut Brain people very difficult. If your Heart Brain is trying to make a connection, there is nothing to connect to, although it can feel the stress in the Gut Brain. A person with an alarmed Gut Brain still has a Heart Brain but it has been walled off. So, your search for compassion, affection, acceptance or even acknowledgement will be fruitless. It means you have to provide safety first.

WHEN A GUT BRAIN FEELS UNSAFE AND BREAKS UP A RELATIONSHIP

What does the unresolved pain of an old relationship do to a new one when the Gut Brain takes Heart Brain decisions?

I had a client in my office who wanted some clarity about a recent breakup. She had instigated the breakup because she felt out of control and was confused by her own behavior. She had for some months a relationship with an amazing guy, whom she described as, "my dream boy, he embodied everything I longed for in my life: loving, caring, adventurous, good-looking, smart, head-spinningly oh, amazing between the sheets and so much more."

Then, she met another person who was almost the opposite, 23 years older than she was, and retired. She had made a decision to pursue a life with him and she was totally puzzled by it. She said, "I just feel so good with this new person. We haven't even got intimate yet, so strange." She wanted to sort out why she had left her dream boy behind, because it did not make sense to her. She described this as: "I just can't help myself, it is out of my control," and, "If I could do it differently, I would."

When we dove into her story, she had had four relationships prior to meeting that dream boy, and all were broken off by her partners, most of whom had run away with somebody else. She said,

"I was always supporting my partners in making their work/career/ life dream happen and when that dream came true, they left me for another partner. Besides causing me heartbreak, I also became a single mom, working long days and always with financial stress. I am so tired of uncertainty. Relationship-wise and materially/future-wise."

In conclusion, her Heart Brain had experienced a lot of betrayal and abandonment.

Her dream boy was actually also pursuing a new career, and was living in another town, too far for daily commuting, and she believed in what he was doing and was also supporting him.

Her new partner was retired, had a good social network in the city where they were living, and did not want to prove anything anymore. Although he was not her type physically and she was not sure if she loved him yet (but she said that could come with time), she felt satisfied with him.

So, when we analyzed what happened, we became aware that her Gut Brain was now making all the decisions. She liked the older man but it was not the love she felt for her dream boy.

The Gut Brain forced her (demonstrated by her words, "I just can't help myself," and, "If I could do it differently, I would") to go with that choice because it would provide safety and stability for her (that is what the Gut Brain lives for). There was no chance of being left behind as she was younger than he, she was a winning lottery ticket for him. In addition, he did not want to push for a new career which could have created the instability of meeting new people who could be seen as a threat. Also, because he was well established in the city, it could help her in her career and therefore towards greater financial stability.

Rule 2: Find the missing need behind their Gut-based behavior/emotion

To have a 'normal adult' conversation when the Gut Brain is activated is practically impossible. It is almost impossible to reach the Head (logic) or the Heart (compassion) while the person is in survival mode. Just think back to the example of the Theological Seminary students — how they stepped over the person who was in need of help. The Gut, as a means of survival, can and will turn off the logic of the Head and the compassion of the Heart.

You can only have that constructive and adult conversation after you/your partner has dealt with the missing need behind the Gut-based behavior/ emotion. So, when we become aware that the Gut Brain is active, we need to connect with the needs that are behind these emotions. Next, we need to ask ourselves, "Can I satisfy this need? Do I want to?" But only after the need is met or the immediacy of the desire has passed can any connection be made on any other level.

Rule 3: Understand the things your partner does or says are not personal.

When your partner's Gut Brain is switched on, and they start communi-cating fear, anger, or rage, or they shut down and stop connecting at all, you must provide **safety** as the first step.

They are sharing these emotions based on their internal scream for safety. So, their internal message is, "Help me, please." Bear in mind that the way in which they communicate will absolutely not sound like that! Remember their Head Brain is turned off, they want to gain control over a situation and their primal survival behaviors are trying to establish that. So, the communication is not filtered through that amazing database upstairs.

So, taking it personally does not help. If we keep our Heart Brain switched on, we could start sensing the need that the other is sharing/screaming at us.

Rule 4: Connect with your own Heart and listen from that place; then use your Head Brain to analyze what's happening with your partner.

The moment you bring your own Gut Brain into the mix, forget a resolution. It will turn into a nasty fight. So, if you have the feeling that your Gut Brain is now more dominant, don't start a discussion. The best thing to do in that moment is to step away, take a five-minute time-out and realign yourself.

Repeat what they said to you, and listen to the words again. Let your head and heart process what it actually means, what the hidden need is.

Rule 5: Decide what to do with the reproductive Gut Brain.

When the reproductive Gut Brain is on, and lust or desire is surfing through the system, then as long that emotion is not satisfied or calmed down, forget about having a normal discussion. Based on your relationship status and willingness, you can decide to go along with it or not. If you aren't interested in connecting on that level, the only option is to walk away.

Rule 6: When you, a friend or partner is hungry or thirsty, take a break to eat or drink.

I am an example of this. When I am hungry or thirsty, I get very grumpy. My partner knows when we are shopping and I say that I would like something to eat or drink, it's best to do this within fifteen minutes, otherwise the shopping experience will become a nightmare full of discussions.

Hungry people's Gut Brain takes over and it's not pretty. There is a reason that 'hangry' has become a commonly understood word.

Rule 7: When you, a friend or partner is really in need of sleep, take a nap and go on the next morning.

I did not put a lot of emphasis on this point and one of our survival needs is also sleep. When people are in a chronically sleep deprived, you can bet that their Gut Brain is active and scanning for the difference between essential needs to be done now and finding ways to postpone or delete the others. If people are chronically sleep deprived their immune system is most of the times diminished.

Can you remember times when you were really in need of sleep and how your social skills were? I guess, at least for me and the many clients who I asked, not the best. The same for solving an argument with your partner just before going to bed when you are sleepy. It is not the best as your Heart Brain is not really active and your Head Brain is also in rest mode. The best solution, hug, kiss, say you are sorry and sleep.

Rule 8: Be aware of the 8 signs of a turned-on Gut Brain

As it has had 500 million years to develop its strategies, the Gut Brain has created many specialized techniques, easily outnumbering those of the Heart Brain or Head Brain.

What are the communication signs of somebody in survival mode?

In psychology, scanning for danger is called the 'orienting response'. You can see this with dogs when they enter a room. They look around, walk about, and scan for the best/safest place to sit or to lie down. We humans have the same Gut Brain programming for these situations as our canine friends, as do other mammals, like rabbits who turn their ears to scan if it's safe.

When you think about the last time you went to a restaurant or a party at a friend's house where you have never been before, what did you or your partner do when you entered? You probably looked around for a nice, safe place to sit. Some people like to sit with their back to the wall because it feels safe, or maybe next to a handsome-looking person with whom we think we could have a good connection.

People who have anxiety issues have their survival Gut Brain on all the time, where their anxiety is related to a fear for the future. That fear could be one or more of many things, for example a presentation they have to give the following day, or a more constant fear like worrying about finances, if they will keep their job, or that they are good enough and no one is criticizing them. How many people do you know who constantly keep their house spick and span, yet when you enter, they still excuse the "mess"? As 10–20% of the Western population is suffering from some degree of anxiety and a staggering 33% will suffer from it sometime in their lives. That means one out of every three couples could experience anxiety in either themselves or their partner.[42]

So, when your partner, for whatever reason, is scanning and they have the idea that something is not okay, their Gut Brain will respond within 10 milliseconds. They may then ask, "Why are you doing that?" (Interrogation based on fear), or a more attack-based response such as, "I don't like what you're doing," based on anger.

When **fear** is more dominant than anger for your partner, you will 9 times out of 10 recognize one of the following communication styles in a 'situation':

1. Your partner becomes silent

Silence, or not responding verbally, is a common strategy because if you don't say anything, there is less reason that somebody will attack you.

This silent strategy can still be witnessed in nature. In nature, when a bear attacks you, the best survival strategy is to play dead on the ground and be silent. The bear will sniff you, maybe push you around; when it has the idea you are dead, it will just walk away.

How many times have you not responded when somebody said something you perceived as an attack, and you thought or were afraid this would become a nasty fight?

2. Your partner starts avoiding the topic or wants to avoid it.

Avoiding means communicating around the issue, starting to talk about another topic, or sometimes also being silent. It results in not really addressing the issue, but instead changing the subject and shifting the focus, using distraction.

How many times did you switch topics because you felt afraid to respond to a question, or to have that talk at that time? Avoiding seemed an easy way out. When the argument is about doing something, avoiding can also mean that you or they will use a lot of excuses to explain why it is not smart/safe, or it is dangerous by summing up all the negatives.

When people are cheating on their partner, you can see this behavior frequently — escaping by changing the subject, or even lying so as not to share the truth and face the painful conversation.

3. They will totally withdraw from the conversation and go away (flee) or be on their own.

Withdrawing means no longer engaging in the conversation. You can see this when people have awkward discussions and feel they are in danger, they 'flee' in some way. A lot of people use this strategy when you want to have a discussion with them — they walk away, start playing on their smartphone, watch TV, go to work, or go back to the 'man cave' as John

Gray said 30 years ago, in his book Men are from Mars, Women are from Venus. Of course, it can just as easily be the woman who withdraws.

You can also see this after breakups, when one partner stops the communication. They may argue that by not being exposed to the other, the healing process is faster. In my professional opinion, it is the opposite. Grieving together about the loss, or supporting the other in the loss and really talking it through, so that all the Brains can fully digest what has happened, has the longest-lasting healing effect. Because this is painful to do, most people withdraw from it and store the trauma in one of their Brains, mostly their Heart Brain. One partner will store the feeling of betrayal or grief of the loss, the other will store the guilt of the actions they did or did not do.

4. Your partner starts placing themselves as a victim, or becomes submissive to seek help from you.

A well-known strategy is playing the victim, which means we act helpless because we feel helpless, and we do our best to attribute an obligation to another person, or play the guilt card so that the other person will help us instead of attacking us. Something like, "You would not hit an old person like me," or, "I'm so tired after a hard day at work, I cannot handle this now, so please don't be hard on me."

Other well-used examples are, "I'm not strong enough; you are a man, you can do that much better," or, "I am a simple guy, and you are a woman; you are much more empathic and a good listener, so it is better that you listen to the story of…"

Using guilt is a form of the victim role that is a widespread strategy. If you watch sitcoms, you will see this stereotyping in a lot of mother characters. It is addressing the Heart Brain of the other; when that person has one, they will be open to this manipulation. However, if they have more of a Gut Brain, they won't care. The words, "If you loved me, you would do that for me," is a great example of a guilt-based strategy, because it suggests that if you don't do something, you are showing that you don't love the other. Sitcoms like The Big Bang Theory often use this stereotyping, especially with Howard's mother.

The submissive form of this strategy is all about pleasing the other person, in the hope that those actions will prevent the other from making them scared or will coerce them into protection. Words like, "Don't be angry, I will do the dishes/clean up/do what you say," are examples of that. In this submissive dominance (SD) scenario, the objective of the submissive person is to receive love and attention as a result of the submissive acts.

You probably have your own examples of the four main fear strategies. Which one does your partner use the most, and which one is more your style?

When somebody is fearful, we need to create safety to bring them back to engage in healthy communication. If the Gut Brain is in charge, the Heart Brain cannot connect to them. And when fear is not the main driver, anger or even rage can be used as other, powerful driving factors.

In a lot of cases, people will move from the fear strategy to the anger strategy; some people skip the fear strategy and go immediately to the anger phase. You can observe this strategy with spiders when you approach them with your finger; instead of running away, they turn around and lift their front legs as if to say, "I'm going to attack you." They skip the fear factor and go instinctively into aggression/attacking mode.

How does our Gut Brain communicate this anger strategy? All of them are different expressions of controlling behavior, and the Gut Brain does its best to coerce others to its way of thinking by using power.

1. Defending, raising the voice and repeating points already made.

What will happen when people are angry or enraged and use a defending tactic? First of all, they will continually repeat their statements to defend their point. They will cut you off, not let you finish a sentence, interrupt you, overstate their facts sometimes with a stronger voice, start speaking in more absolute terms (black and white), generalize more, and attempt to dominate the conversation. At this point, they can also become silent or withdrawn, in order to shut you out, so they could say, "I am not talking to you anymore." Although it sounds similar to fear, in the fear state they still want you to connect; while in this defending state, they do not want to connect. Refer back to the examples of anxious and avoiding behavior in toddlers (see Section 5: How do the Three Brains work for young people?).

2. Attacking, by criticizing, judging, and blaming others.

The attacking strategy employs these communication styles:

a. To label/stereotype and generalize
b. To criticize the other person or their thoughts

Maybe this has happened to you too: Your partner is showing you something they made. And from a positive interest you ask, "Why did you do this; I know you are extremely busy with work?" or, "Who told or asked you to do this?"

A 'why' question is asking for the deeper motivation or values of someone, so it could trigger an open Gut Brain nerve, and your partner could feel judged or questioned because of your reasoning.

And instead of a nice answer, you get:

• You're always questioning why I do things! Don't you think I can make my own decisions?
• Because I thought it would be helpful. You never support my ideas.

- Because I thought it was a good idea. You always criticize my ideas.
- Nobody did, this is my own idea, why is it not good enough? Are you the only one who can do it?
- My colleague/my friends, and I trust them, and at least they support me.
- You asked me to do this two weeks ago, don't you remember? You never pay attention to what we discuss.

Or without defending, straight away going for the kill:

- Why did you do this?
- You probably would not understand. It is rather advanced and complicated.
- Should I first ask your permission to do something?
- Who told you to do this?
- Nobody, I decided all by myself, isn't it amazing?
- Not my mother! Why are you asking?

Have you ever got a response like this, or maybe responded in this way?

a. Label/stereotype/generalize: The moment a person labels, stereotypes, or generalizes something or somebody, they want to place the other person, or their thoughts, in a subset of the real world, so that the other's suggestions are not applicable to this situation for them.

As an example, you may be talking about cleaning the house, and your partner starts arguing that house does not have to be "OCD clean". This then means that all your arguments about how the house in which you both live should be maintained are no longer valid, because you and your actions are labelled 'OCD'.

b. Criticizing: "You sound just like your mother/father." Criticizing goes one step further, because it is a global condemnation of a person's behavior.

So, in this state, the person may roll their eyes, start looking at their watch, or, shake their head in disagreement, and say, "You never listen, you are really selfish and insensitive," or, "You are not a good mother/partner." You can identify this when they put a global statement on you regarding who they think you are, in other words, an extreme judgment of you.

3. Belittling (contempt), placing themselves in the position of authority and putting the other person down

This is one of the worst ways you can be treated. Belittling, also called 'contempt', means the other person places themselves in a position of authority and puts you down. This is a painful step further down the ladder in really connecting with the other person, or having a loving relationship, and is horrendous for your relationship. In criticizing, it is more about your behavior; in belittling, it is more about your character.

The objective of this strategy is to make you feel small, unimportant, and insignificant, while they place themselves on a stool of wisdom by being better than you, showing that they are on higher ground.

Some examples of belittling are:

- "That's just female talk."
- "Do you have your period again?"
- "What you're saying is stupid."
- "You are being childish."
- "Men don't have a heart, so how can you ever feel love?"
- Men only think with their d****, and that is really a small Brain, especially yours."
- "The only thing females are good at is producing children and being in the kitchen, and you are also a bad cook."
- "Which university did you go to, did you have any education at all?"
- "Females don't know what it's like to be in a real fight."
- "If you never experienced it, you don't know what you're talking about."

And, of course, racism and discrimination are further examples of this hurtful strategy.

Does this behavior ring any bells for you? If it does, it is an extremely serious signal to start re-evaluating your relationship. There is a huge chance you are on a sinking ship.

Gottman, a worldwide recognized specialist in relationships and communication between couples, concluded after years of research that the real killer in a relationship is placing yourself in a better position than the other, hence belittling or contempt. He concluded that 99% of the couples who use this strategy will divorce or break up sooner or later.[43]

When your partner speaks from a superior place, it's very damaging, and belittling or contempt is any statement made from a higher level. A lot of the time it's an insult or a power position, e.g., "I am better than you, and you are nothing," or, "I'm the boss so you should do this," or, "I'm the parent so you should do that," or, "I am married to you so I can say that," or, "You are a bitch. You're scum." The person saying these things is trying to put the other on a lower level than they really are. This hierarchical behavior is poisonous in a relationship.

Using anger, and the other strategies mentioned, has become normalized. We need look no further than US politics and the elections; it is 'normal' to attack your opponent with all means at your disposal. Insult, blame, and contempt are all used and accepted in order to win votes. For the former US president, Donald Trump, it was his favorite strategy; and yes, it was an extremely successful one too. He became president with this strategy, so it's natural that people start copying it; when the US president is doing it, it must be normal to do so. You can find other examples in the business world, as it is now considered rational behavior in several industries.

4. Threatening, punishing the other person, physical actions

The last tactic is physical attack: threatening or physical violence. Although it's not in Gottman's research, I think we can agree that this violates every boundary of typical conversations or relationships, and for me it is unacceptable without any discussion. It is time to run away from your relationship if this happens!

This tactic is used by someone who enters into a rage, with the objective to emotionally or physically hurt the other so much that they will give up and agree with them. This can be seen in statements such as, "If you do that, I will tell your friends/parents, I will share it on Facebook, Instagram, Snapchat, etc., and your life will be a living hell after that," or, "Stop it or I will give you a slap/hit you/hurt you." They may threaten to kill you, or even not use words, but actually carry out the violent behavior. Rape is also part of this behavior. Statistics suggest that this tactic is unfortunately commonly used in relationships (threatening happens more and more on social media where the sender can be anonymous).

If any of these types of threatening or physical behavior is happening to you, my advice is to leave your partner, let the police deal with them, and find your happiness elsewhere. Your partner needs serious help and that is not your responsibility. These people have so much internal pain that their only option in discussions is to create pain for the other, not because it is their intention, but this is the only strategy they know. Sadly, they probably experienced and learned the behavior from a young age, and with all your good intentions, you cannot help them, you will only hurt yourself in the process. I have seen too many clients who tried and got badly burned.

The most important thing to remember is that their anger is not directed at you (so please do not take it personally, there is nothing wrong with you), even if their behavior is. You could say that when somebody expresses this fear strategy, they still have 'hope' somewhere that you are willing to help them. When they express anger/rage, they learned at some point that they cannot trust another person to help them or save them, so they need to win. Therefore, making them aware that you are not the enemy besides creating safety for them is essential, but still, you are not their therapist!

If your partner has an active Gut Brain and is using aggression as the default response, simple conversations can go wrong, even though you didn't do anything particular to aggravate the situation.

In extreme cases, usually when the relationship involves violence, the partner who receives the violence can be so extremely threatened and fearful that (mostly it is the women who have to endure this, but it can be the man too) they enter a shutdown phase and do not dare (are even physically unable) to leave their violent partner. They have sadly given up hope that they can escape this violent situation.

EXAMPLE: A COMMON SITUATION OF MISUNDERSTANDING FOR COUPLES:

A couple come home after a day at work, physically and/or mentally tired.

For Gut Brain people, the Gut Brain will be very much in charge at this point. We now know its main objective is keeping the boss safe. When in desperate need of rest and rejuvenation, it is all about 'Me' at that moment.

Being a loyal soldier, the Gut Brain advises the boss to have a little rest, sit on the couch, watch some television, check social media, have a drink and maybe a bite to eat, or just do nothing, zone out. It employs strategies like being silent, avoiding, withdrawing, and remaining disconnected from others.

And now, imagine the partner is more of a Heart Brain person; when they come home tired, they rejuvenate by connecting. A Heart Brain person creates safety by connecting with others. This means they like to start talking, share what happened during the day, what a colleague said to the boss, how the boss responded, what the colleague thought/felt of it, and how they had to talk to the Heart Brain person to overcome their disappointment and sadness.

For the Gut Brain person, this is almost a fatal attack; the boss is in a weak spot, like a turtle laying on his back, and the Gut Brain believes the Heart Brain person is going to attack them, kill them, eat them, help .... And takes suitable action.

The resulting scenarios originate from a fear attitude or an attack and can be: "I need a rest so please shut up"; "Call your friends or mother, I'm watching TV" (and turning up the TV); "Can I have a break, I've been working really hard, when you're tired I leave you alone, how come you cannot do that for me?" Or actions such as walking away to get a drink out of the fridge and going to another room. If they go more into victim mode, they might say, "Please leave me alone, I'm tired," and then use a soft, whining voice.

The husband of a couple I once saw told me, "When my partner comes home, I just close my eyes and put a post-it on my chest with the text, 'Recharging battery, please don't disturb me until dinner's ready."

And it is clear what will happen next if the Heart Brain person does not understand which of their partner's Brains is in control. The Heart Brain person could feel rejected, not understood, not taken care of and maybe/probably thinks, "My partner does not love me anymore." At that moment, the Gut Brain will support the Heart to deal with the perceived threat. When that happens, the Gut Brain could step in to protect the broken heart and use one of the Gut Brain strategies to protect the Heart.

The Heart Brain person's response could then be one of the following: "I'm also tired, you are extremely insensitive," or, "You were home earlier than I was, why didn't you cook, you know I love it when you take care of me," or, "You never listen to me when I would like to share something."

If the Heart Brain wants to create a drama, it may say something like, "My parents warned me about you," or, "You don't love me anymore," or start crying, or say 'hate' words.

The Heart Brain person could start to communicate even more, based on the lost connection, and when the Heart Brain person starts talking more to reconnect, the partner's Gut Brain will become even more alarmed and disconnect even further.

If the Gut Brain person is smart, and connects with their own Heart Brain, they could respond, "That is horrible what happened. I've missed you all day, and I am happy to see you. Please could you share this story while we have dinner?"

The four rules of dealing with Head Brains: understand before being understood

When we speak about the Head Brain, there are four main emotions, if we can call them emotions. Our beautiful Head Brain can spark up curiosity, interest, surprise and disagreement, all with the intention to learn more, in order to improve our prediction of the future and our chances of survival.

Misunderstandings arise when your partner's Head Brain logic is different from yours. Disagreement or rejection then step in.

I was once biking to the shopping center with a friend, who is a strong Head Brain-oriented person. The most logical route was to follow the bike path to the shopping center, which goes around a little hill in the middle of the village. At a traffic light, I said to him, "Let's go over the hill, it's a better way."

'Better' is a judgment that means comparing one option to another. So, he asked, "Why it is better?" I responded, "Because it's shorter and in a straight line." His reply was, "But it means going over the hill, so it is actually longer and will take more time." (Logically, he and his Head Brain were right)

I gave it a second shot and said, "It's also something different, we always bike this way." He bounced back with, "Then it is not better, just different."

At that moment, I reconnected with myself and thought about what I had said at the start of the discussion. When I used the word 'better', I had activated his logical Head Brain. I had made a comparison, and his logic had stepped in. So, I rephrased my sentence and said that what I wanted to propose was to take the hill because, although it's a little bit more biking, the off-road experience would be more fun. It would also allow us to see how the sunflowers are growing on the hill and enjoy the beautiful spring view.

So, I changed from the judgment 'better' to what I meant when I thought of 'better'. I thought of all the positives of changing the route — more fun, some nice moments of joy and beauty — but I had originally only communicated my end conclusion as a judgment. I observed my friend thinking, weighing up the options of fun versus logic, and, with a big smile, he also decided to take the hill.

Rule 1: Understand their logic first

When you have a discussion or a misunderstanding with a Head Brain person, it is essential to understand their logic first, and how they came to the conclusion that they did. If you know that, you can work with it. If not, it becomes a struggle.

As the "fear" of the Head Brain is to be wrong, or to have knowledge or work criticized. That means that to let the Head Brain be open for discussion we first need to know their point of view.

If you do not know where they are coming from, everything you say can and will be used against you, as their logic does not fit yours.

Rule 2: Every generalization/judgment creates a disagreement or rejection response

If you would like to propose or discuss something with a Head Brain person, be aware that every judgment that you make about their logic could produce an argument. If your logic does not match their logic, stick to the facts. When a Head Brain person thinks you're "attacking/judging" their logic, it could and probably will activate their Gut Brain and you will be lost in translation.

I'm using the term 'judgment' here to mean a comparison between two alternatives, and judging or labelling one alternative better than the other.

What happens is that the other person must accept your judgment, or your view on the world, whilst you are putting their opinion aside.

To simplify this, just imagine for the moment that we are going to apply the Dutch rule of communication everywhere in the world. The Dutch communicate straight to the point: "Say what you think, even if it hurts the other person, because according to our Dutch view, a way of showing respect is to be bluntly honest." When this reasoning is applied, the Dutch is the best way.

When you read this: "Showing respect = Being totally honest, therefore the Dutch way is the best," how does your Head Brain respond?

I could assume that you think this is blunt, stupid, arrogant, wrong and is the opposite to showing respect and more. Hence you reject my point of view and that makes sense because by stating it like this I do not respect your view on this.

Furthermore, what happens in your body? It could be that you even feel rejection there.

Even when it's entirely logical for us, it doesn't mean it's logical for the other person.

Just think a moment about all the things you find logical, but your partner does not or vice versa? Just imagine you had to agree with all his/her quirky logic?

Everything you and your partner have experienced/learned is stored in your/their Head Brain memory and when it is believed to be valid as a rule, this can be a potential landmine when you start imposing it on the other.

I truly believe, based on all my experience, that the most important rule for really connecting with your partner is: **No judging**, but instead observe and listen with your heart and find the needs that are missing as a couple.

The moment you make a judgment about how something should be, e.g., using words like "it is", "always", "it should", "never" etc., or expressing what is different from your personal opinion and how you think it should be, you are creating a generalization and expect that your partner will start sharing your world view, values, and decisions.

Now just turn the tables. Are you willing to accept the judgments and generalizations of your partner, and live according to those rules? I assume, and truly hope, not.

When we believe we have the right to our own opinion (and I believe that is normal), we are also obliged to respect that right for our partner.

Rule 3: When your two logic systems disagree, explain the steps for how you got to your conclusion and be aware of their Gut Brain reaction

As the 'standard' reaction is disagreement or rejection, it is necessary to go step by step through the process so that the other person's Head Brain can follow your logic, instead of just having to accept the outcome. Be aware that a Head Brain can accept facts to change its mind, but it will not do as well with opinions or just thoughts. It needs logical proof!

Rule 4: be aware of the signs of a blocked Head Brain

Although the Head Brain is easy as it is analytical without emotions it can still be blocked and be less willing to listen to you. Most of the time this happens when the Heart or Gut Brain is directing the head as they disagree.

The Head Brain can be blocked by itself when it has a strong conviction that what it knows is right!

The sign that this is the happening is when your partner is too critical, or too judgmental, or too much of a perfectionist.

The six rules of dealing with Heart Brains: stay connected

As the Heart Brain is the 'Us' brain, you may assume it is easier to connect and deal with the Heart Brain person. It is and is not at the same time, because they are sensitive to fake communication, therefore both partners have to be on the same connection level.

Rule 1: The Heart Brain wants to feel connected and hates rejection.

As the Heart Brain is the 'Us' brain and despises rejection, a break up could break their heart. It also means that if communication is not on a frequent basis (whatever their idea is of 'frequent'), they could feel rejected.

In all cases when we talk about connection and how to deal with a Heart Brain person, it is worth remembering that the Heart Brain is connected via the ventral vagal nerve and the cranial nerves to most facial muscles including our eye muscles, and the muscles in the middle ear, so is sensitive to actions such as smelling, swallowing, smiling, frowning, listening, and eye movements.

Why is this important to remember?

It means that when communicating with a Heart person in particular, but also with a Gut person, texting is not the best way to share a 'heavy' topic. The Heart Brain wants to feel connected.

The Heart Brain person likes to have physical connection, to see, hear, or feel you, and feels a bit disconnected when it is only through text.

When there is an issue, they want to talk!

Rule 2: The Heart Brain person wants to feel it is about 'Us' and doesn't like to only hear about your needs.

It means listening to the Heart Brain person, giving them space to express their needs, emotions and feelings. Listening to a Heart Brain person is one of the most beautiful gifts you can give them. As it shows them that you are connected.

Rule 3: For the Heart Brain person, texting is reading that you still care for them, but emotional topics are best discussed in person.

It is so easy to text, "I love you", or send a heart emoticon, while not really feeling it while you type.

One of the main reasons for this is that when we text, we do not use those nerves and muscles from the face that are connected to our heart. Similarly, you cannot predict what the other person's emotional state will be when they read it. Also, when we read, we do not use all the cranial nerves that are connected to our heart unless you take the trouble to hand write a (love) letter; this shows effort made, and when the recipient reads it, they are guided into a similar state as yours when you wrote it.

This means, on the flip side, it is easier to write/text stronger statements to your partner than you would say in person. So, it is easier to create tension in this way. Also, a Heart Brain person does not really feel the emoticons in a text message.

EXAMPLE: HOW IT GOES WRONG WHEN A HEAD BRAIN IS TEXTING A HEART BRAIN

Once I had an argument with a friend of mine. In my opinion, she was being conservative (this is a judgment and was my first mistake because this is a Gut Brain judgment), she did not share her feelings and I was feeling frustrated (again, my Gut Brain in action) about that.

What did I do? I analyzed that I was emotional, so went up two levels to the Head Brain. It gave me the advice to be logical and to explain to my friend how I observed the conversation and how I felt about it.

So, I sent her a message on WhatsApp, which was mistake number one from my Head Brain (not to consult the other Brains for advice on what to do). It felt safer to send a WhatsApp message, as I wouldn't then have to deal with her emotional state — Gut Brain logic — and we only needed to communicate with words.

In the message, I logically explained what I observed, what I felt, what my need was and what my request was.

I thought I had followed all the steps for perfect communication. I probably would have been right had we had the conversation in person. Instead, it was a one-way conversation, a brain dump of my analysis.

The second mistake of the Head Brain: To address my point and make the right analytical assumption from my side, I added some parts of previous conversations we had had, and I explained what my assumption was based on. Although my intention was to create a logical overview, it was perceived by her as condescending (her Heart Brain felt rejected and her Gut Brain attacked).

What do you think the response was, knowing that she is more a Heart Brain person? Yes, a total explosion of frustration, with her demanding to know why I was lecturing her like one of my students or clients, and that she did not need any coaching or therapy done on her.

I think we have all had such experiences at least once in our lives. Especially nowadays with WhatsApp and texting taking over verbal communication and real-life interaction, the chance of such an experience is increasing.

The real Head Brain person will do their utmost to explain in procedural steps what the observation is about and what's happening between them, and will also explain to the partner which protocol could be used for the situation. It is almost like discussing an Excel spreadsheet or a profit and loss statement while talking about human interaction. We are turning human connection into a series of robotic steps and procedures.

What should I have done differently, knowing that she was a Heart Brain person?

I should have called her and expressed somehow that my heart needed attention, or that I missed the real her and wanted to hear what was going on in her life, and to let me be part of that.

It is good to know that, as a rule of thumb, the Head Brain loves text messages.

Why? Because it is easy, quick and you don't need a real connection with somebody. You can also take time to think logically about what you want to write and not write, and you will not hear the other person's reaction immediately. Communication between two people using email or text is seen by the Head Brain as a safe option.

Rule 4: A Heart Brain person loves to hear every day that you still care about them.

As connection is key for them, they love to hear that and feel that it is still there.

Metaphorically, just as dogs will always welcome each other when they meet, Heart Brain people love to do the same.

Rule 5: "Sorry" is a great word to hear for a Heart Brain person.

A Heart Brain person loves to hear an apology when you are wrong, so that they feel they are still connected.

Rule 6: The signs the Heart Brain is disconnected

Just like your Head or Gut Brains the Heart Brain can be disconnected or not open for connection.

The strongest signs that they are not open for our words or connection is when they show signs of indifference or hatred.

Indifference shows up in different ways and sometimes it is hard to distinguish the difference between a Gut brain response like: "I am now taking care of myself" and the Heart Brain behavior of "I don't want to engage with you." The main distinction between both is that when it is indifference the person is not taking an action that has the objective to benefit themselves, they just don't want to engage with you even when it means they are worse off. The reasoning behind this is that according to them you breached some extremely important rules of engagement or values.

15.

The seven essential steps to really connect with the other person

So how do you bring yourself to that state of being connected, how do you make it fit, how do you really connect with your partner?

Step 1: Get aligned within yourself

Although it is not always easy, especially when we are triggered, the first step is to become aware of your own emotional state. If you are mainly in your Head, Heart, or Gut, it means you are not aligned, and that could cause misinterpretations. Being aware of the needs of your partner, can you detect which Brain is in action now and what the underlying needs are?

How do you do that? When you text, call, or talk to someone, take a moment before or after to become aware of which of your Brains was most active. In this way, you will train yourself to detect your own patterns.

Train yourself to never respond right away when you feel your Gut Brain jump up. The good thing is that intensity of these sensations fade if you act within 5 seconds of being aware of them. Biologically speaking the amygdala is triggered and sends out the neurotransmitters to activate us and this lasts for 5 seconds. If we do nothing to stop the perceived trigger it will activate the adrenal glands. The neurotransmitters are then released into the bloodstream and that can last up to 5 hours. It is therefore important to know how to act in those first 5 seconds. When the trigger hits: immediately take a deep breath, expand your belly whilst inhaling and breath out slowly via your nose for relaxation. When you start doing this after the 5 seconds, continue doing this for a further 10 to 20 times until you feel connected with yourself again. The inhalation and exhalation rhythm will rebalance your Three Brains via the (para)sympathetic never system.

Remember: When you are in an emotional state, you will make emotional decisions and they will have emotional outcomes.

Step 2: Which Brain is talking?

Ask yourself, what were the words I heard or read? Repeat them to yourself by saying them out loud in a neutral voice.

Check which words were used, check with chapter 11: How to find out: which Brain is talking? The language and words of our Three Brains for the references. And when you speak out the words feel inside with of your Brains would be in charge of these words.

So, you can really become aware which of the Brains is talking, and be either upset or at ease. You can also be aware which ones are silent.

Step 3: Which Brain is "upset" and which Brains are, okay?

After you know which of the Brains is talking then it is essential to find the Brain that is having the "issue".

To analyze this, the most important thing to do is objectively categorise from the words being used, to which Brain they belong and if the intention of that sentence is that they are communicating in solution mode, or in a protection mode. By protection mode I mean that they don't want to change.

Sometimes you find this explained in other literature as saboteurs, villains or other negative narratives. Another important thing to know is that everything our Brains do is coming from a positive intention. This does not mean that the behavior demonstrated or outcome is positive. We learned this coping behavior a long time ago when it was useful to stay connected or keep us safe. For some valid reasons we never changed that coping behavior.

Examples of solution (supporting) mode:

- I understand it but … (Head Brain)
- I still like you but … (Heart Brain)
- I like it but … (Gut Brain)

Examples of protection mode:

- It is stupid … , or you don't (want to) understand me … (Head Brain)
- I cannot look at you … or you don't (or never) like(d) my family…. (Heart Brain)
- You never support me … or I cannot trust you (Gut Brain)

The following example scenario will help you to understand how to distinguish the patterns. Imagine that you have a discussion with your partner about weight loss after visiting the doctor. The doctor shared: "It's really serious, you need to lose weight!". This is how a Gut, Heart and Head-Brain dominant partner could respond:

The typical Gut-Brain responses:
In supporter mode:

- I need to lose weight for my health.
- I don't want to end up in a hospital.

- I have a diagnosis of (pre-)type 2 diabetes. I'm terrified the condition will tremendously affect my life.
- I don't want to take medication and look vulnerable.

In protector mode:

- I had an upbringing where we never had enough food.
- We ate beans, rice, or bread the last week of the month.
- I ate the school breakfast if it was available.
- I feel good, and my family is alive. When they die, it will be due to old age.

The typical Heart-Brain responses:

In supporter mode

- I love my kids and want to be an example, so I'd like to be healthy.
- As a grandparent, I'd love to be there for my grandchildren as they grow up, therefore, healthy eating is important.
- I want to enjoy life, so I'd like to adjust my unhealthy habits.

In protector mode:

- My family is Italian; meals are social occasions, eating brings us together.
- I can't leave my family to take care of myself.
- My mum loves to cook, and to love her means eating her food.
- I like to enjoy life and have fun with my friends over meals.

The typical Head-Brain responses:

In supporter mode:

- I don't have the healthiest lifestyle, and I could change my eating habits.
- My friends have made health changes, and I could learn from them.
- I know I overeat and don't exercise enough.

In protector mode:

- I don't know how to change my unhealthy routine. I have a busy life, family, kids, and work.
- I don't know how to find time to exercise or shop for healthier food.
- I don't know which healthy food choices I should buy. I think everything is full of fat and sugar.
- I don't know how to shop, prepare, or cook healthy food

Step 4: Analyze which needs your partner is expressing that they would like to have met.

The golden rules are that every one of our Three Brains have their own needs–see chapter 5: Our Three Brains' strengths and weaknesses.

The ultimate highest needs are:

- The Head Brain needs to understand and agree with it,
- The Heart Brain wants to be connected and
- The Gut Brain wants to be safe.

And everything we say or do is actually an expression to achieve that. Even though the words that are used may be totally different than expressing these needs.

As Marshall Rosenberg says in his book Nonviolent Communication,[44] people say only two things: "Please" and "Thank you." This seems hard to believe, but it is true, and people have amazing abilities to hide their true message.

When the Gut Brain is on, they say *please* make the situation safe, *please* fulfill my desires/lust, and *please* provide me with nurturing food or drink, or they say *thank you* for doing so. When somebody says: "Are you stupid, can't you see I'm taking a nap, watching TV etc.?" what they really want to express is, "Please could you give me some time so I can rejuvenate because I'm tired?"

When the Heart Brain is in charge, they say **please** let's connect or **thank you** for connecting with me, which means if your partner says, "You are never home," what they want to express is, "Please, I would love to see you a little bit more this week. Shall we spend the evening together?"

When the Head Brain is behind the steering wheel, it says **please** explain it to me again, or a **thank you** for explaining it again or listening to my explanation.

As an example, "What you are saying is total crap," actually means, "Please could you explain it again, because according to my logic it does not fit?"

If you get the idea, "So I should bend over backwards to understand my partner, but they can still be a jerk at communication." that is not my intended meaning. As Stephen Covey wrote in the book The 7 Habits of Highly Effective People,[45] seek first to understand, then to be understood.

A way for you to become aware of the hidden needs are is to test how your different Brains interpret this message.

A nice way to exercise this is to place your own fingers on your Head, Heart, or Gut, as in the exercise we did earlier, and repeat the exact words of your partner, not your idea of what they said, but the exact words, and ask your Head, Heart, and Gut what they make of it.

The moment you verbalize your interpretation of what your partner said, it is already processed by your Gut, Head, and Heart Brains. And if the first or second is in charge, you can almost be sure a judgment (from the Gut a negative protective one and from the Head it may be a logical one) is placed on it, and that you missed your partner's meaning and need/s that were expressed.

Step 5: The essential questions, to find solutions to the missing needs

Questions you can ask your partner when you believe the Gut Brain is in protection mode:

- What do you need to feel safe and trusted to allow us to go on with …
- What do you need from me to feel secure that I am 100% on your side?
- If I asked: "What happens if you would follow your gut feeling to complete objectives," what would you say or do?

Questions you can ask your partner when you believe the Heart Brain is in protection mode:

- What do you need to feel not rejected by me?
- What do you need to feel appreciated by me?
- If I asked: " What happens if you would follow your Heart," what would you say or do?
- What support does your Heart need to achieve the objective?

Questions you can ask your partner when you believe the Head Brain is in protection mode:

- What do you need from me to know I understand you?
- What is it that you want me to understand?
- If I asked: " What happens when you think this through," what would you say or do?

Step 6: Listen which needs your partner is expressing that they would like to have met.

What are the needs behind their message? And ask clarification questions to really get a clear picture of the needs of your partner.

By using empathetic listening to genuinely understand a person, you compel them to reciprocate the listening and take an open mind which can then be influenced by you. This creates an atmosphere of caring, and positive problem-solving. The interesting fact is that this fifth habit is greatly embraced in the Greek philosophy of 2,500 years ago and represented by three words:

Ethos is your personal credibility. It's the trust that you inspire, based on your own values of integrity.

Pathos is the empathetic side. It's the alignment with the emotional trust of another person in communication.

Logos is the logic, the reasoning part of the presentation.

If you are not willing to understand your partner, then why would your partner have the same intention? When we stay in the 'Me-first' zone, it becomes a competition. The Gut Brain is taking over the driver's seat and we now know where the drive will lead us, don't we?

When we are able to create a healthy connection and find out the need behind their behavior or communication — what your partner is missing that creates that feeling of being unsafe, rejected, misunderstood and so on — it is more likely than not that the solution will present itself without even asking for it. I don't know how it is with you, but when I think about all the discussions, I have had with somebody else or the discussions I have observed in my client room or training room, more than 95% of the time, we discuss and fight over the symptoms, instead of what it is really about.

Step 7: Decide if you are willing and able to fulfill those.

Step 8: Communicate back from your Heart. It can be a yes or no, but it must be done with compassion.

Steps to respond are:

1. *Am I correct that what I hear that your needs are…?*

2. *Thank you for sharing that with me*

3. *It makes me feel/gives me the impression that this is what you expect from me…*

4. *So, what I can do is…*

5. *And what I cannot do is…*

6. *How could this work for you?*

So, what to do when you are not in the mood, you are also tired or busy with work or things that require your Head Brain to be in action? The solution is sometimes extremely easy! Spend 10 minutes to connect with your Heart Brain or let the Gut Brain rejuvenate and relax for 10-20 minutes to find the perfect solution; go for a walk to change your physiology if you have spent the entire day at the office in front of a screen.

Essentially, you must establish a safe environment for yourself, because when your Gut Brain is active, it can perceive everything as an attack and do anything to protect you, the boss. From that safe environment, we can start connecting with the need our partner's Gut Brain has; the need that is missing at that moment, and the reason why the Gut Brain is active and on alert. Of course, we can ask for the need, but as we are already aware, even questions can be perceived as an attack when we don't really create a safe environment first. To let the Heart Brain become active, the Gut Brain must feel safe. So, usually the best thing to do in these circumstances is to guess the need, and then ask if you're right about it, and how you can support that need for your partner and yourself.

EXAMPLE: REAL LIFE APPLICATION OF THE THREE BRAINS THEORY

1. *"Hi honey!" Use your usual term of endearment. That sends out the signal that you love them and that your intention is good. It creates a feeling of safety for the other person. Think back to a time when you were young, and your mother or father called you by your full name, can you remember how that felt? That is precisely the opposite of what we want to achieve.*

2. *"I see you're sitting on the couch…" (observation) and not an interpretation, like: "I see you being lazy on the couch," (Gut Brain talking)*

3. *"…and I wonder if your need is to have a rest and regain your energy before, we do something else or talk about how our day was." By asking for the needs of the Gut Brain, the Gut Brain feels it is acknowledged and understood. That's a vital step in creating safety for the Gut Brain. You talk directly to it.*

Before we even verbalize our needs or wishes, it could be good to think about these three questions:

- *What do you really want for yourself in this communication?*
- *What do you really want for the other person in this communication?*
- *What do you really want for the relationship in this communication?*

When you have that clear, think about the best way to communicate your needs and wishes.

Why are these three steps important? Because there is a difference between:

"I want for myself to be able to express my needs and you should understand my needs," and,

"My request to you is that you really listen to me, acknowledge me by summarizing or repeating what I said, and please think and feel about what I said before you respond. And if I was not clear in what I told you so that you did not understand what I meant; then could you please ask a question for clarification?"

I know this is a mouthful and it doesn't have to be word for word, but if you do not communicate what your needs are, you will not get what you want.

It is like going to a restaurant and asking the waiter to bring something to drink. How well do you think the waiter knows what you really want to drink? It could be sparkling water, a wine, a beer, or a coke etc. We find it totally normal to tell the waiter what we want, so why don't we think it's normal to do the same with our partner?

When you ask for water, the waiter will ask you whether you want tap water, flat, sparkling, with ice or a slice of lemon, because his job is to understand your needs. Otherwise, he will bring the wrong thing. To expect the same from your partner, they need to be in the mood to do so.

I wonder how many times you've said, "Just listen to me," or, "You don't listen." I know I have said this when my partner did not understand me, until I realized how it feels when somebody says that to you. It becomes something totally different if you say, "I would like to share my opinion, thoughts or feelings and would really appreciate it if you would do your best to listen to me and understand what I would like to share with you."

Section 5:

FOR WHEN YOU HAVE CHILDREN, HOW DO THEIR THREE BRAINS WORK?

16.

Children also have Three Brains (But only two are booted up)

How children's Brains develop

One unique thing about human beings is that we are equipped with Brains so large and so complex that they take years for our bodies to build them. Those bodies are developed enough to survive outside of the womb after gestating only about 40 weeks. Those nine months can seem an eternity, for sure. But they're nothing when you grasp how long it takes for a Brain to fully develop.

Scientists have determined that not one of our Three Brains is fully formed until we are over twenty years old![46] Before we start calling the Homo sapiens customer support line, demanding to be sent infants with completely formed Brains, let's appreciate the reasons that we, unlike our more cognitively simple animal relations, are born as works-in-progress. One big reason is that, if our heads got any bigger in utero, we would not fit down the birth canal. And we would almost certainly kill our mothers if we tried.

Those large heads, combined with the skeletal adaptations we had to make to walk erect, are the biggest reasons that, in times past, giving birth placed women in mortal peril. The number of women who died in childbirth before the advent of modern medicine, and the emergency alternative of Caesarean section, is staggering and appalling. Even today, in a place like Afghanistan where women give birth at home and in their villages, one woman in eleven will die in childbirth.[47]

A second, and crucial reason that our Brains are born only partially formed is that they are designed to build themselves based on their experiences and stimuli. How does this work? Like this: When, as a newborn, people talk to you, your brain sets about creating the structures that process language. When you are taught to sing or make music, the brain structures that process music (and, not coincidentally, mathematics) grow. With those new hard-wired structures, you can process rhythms, timing, tone and patterns better and more quickly. And doing things better, more quickly, and perceiving more subtleties about the world around us is what Head Brains, especially, evolved to do. Coming to understandings more quickly and with more insight is in fact, the definition of 'intelligence'.

What happens to people who are deprived of such stimulation? Tragically, we do know. Brain scan studies of children who were raised without anyone speaking to them — like some who were raised in Eastern Block "orphanages" — make clear the terrible impact of depriving a child of stimulation, especially in their earliest years. Many children in those horrible institutions went years without being held or spoken to. So now we know what happens. If a child is not spoken to and taught to speak in their first few years of life, the Brain structures that process language do not develop. In the scans, you can see that those centers are missing from their Brains. To make matters worse, once the window of time in which that structure needs to be created passes, it is too late. No amount of therapy can create a cognitive structure that does not exist.

As we have discussed in earlier chapters, those capacious and supple Brains are what allowed us to lose many of the things that, in our earlier evolutionary careers as animals, were crucial to survival. Sharp teeth and fur were made unnecessary by Brains that could use tools, build shelters and make clothing. We evolved the capacity to acquire the necessities of survival, not with physical adaptations, but intellectual power. As we evolved, we also gained the ability to communicate, to plan, to cook, to calculate and to trade. Instead of doing all the work ourselves, we learned to exploit other animals, the natural world and, of course, one another. Along the way, those teeth and claws became unnecessary, or too biologically expensive to maintain. (Even Mother Nature operates on a budget. If you want to spend your energy budget on a big brain, then there are other things you just don't have the resources for.)

Children's Brains are different

So how do we apply what we have learned about our Three Brains to interact and communicate with people whose Gut, Heart and Head Brains are developing at different speeds? Children's Three Brains are learning not only about the world and how to interact with it, but how to communicate and negotiate with one another, and mostly how to stay connected with the caregivers. To top it all off, their Three Brains are constantly changing and the balance between them is changing too. The Brain that rules the roost at the age of three may be playing second fiddle at five. Or, even, at three-and-a-half. In fact, the Brain that's running the show in the morning may be nowhere to be found by late afternoon.

So how do we hope to understand and communicate with creatures whose Brains are in constant flux?

There are, of course, entire libraries devoted to looking at these questions, but how can our three-Brain insights help us understand and communicate with our own children? In fact, understanding how the Three Brains form, change and interact in childhood could be a profoundly important help in improving communication with the children in our world. Not only that, and possibly more importantly, it can help us guide and shape our children's experiences so that they avoid some of the emotional and cognitive disconnections that can make adult's lives so filled with fear and anxiety.

First, let's go over some of the things we know. After that, we can get to the question of applying that knowledge to our child-rearing and child-communication strategies.

Gestation

In the first weeks after conception, our gut and Gut Brain develop at astonishing speed. From a couple of cells, we develop our system for digesting food, and millions and millions of nerve cells are created to communicate with all the other organs and with the Head Brain.[48]

By the seventh week of gestation, the neural crest cells have colonized the entire gut — in short, the Gut Brain develops first[49] ahead of the development of the Heart and Head Brain neurons. In fact, those cells that started creating the intestines and nerve cells in the abdomen are the ones that replicate and become the ventral and dorsal vagus nerve, the spine, and the other Brains. So, our Head and Heart Brains are the Eves fashioned from the rib of parent cells from our gut and Gut Brain.

The creation of the human Head Brain from the tip of a 3-millimeter neural tube is a marvel of biological engineering. To arrive at the 100 billion plus neurons that are the standard equipment of a newborn baby, the Head Brain of a developing child in the womb grows at an average rate of about 250,000 nerve cells per minute.[50]

So, what happens after we are born, and why is that so important in relation to the Three Brains Theory? Because to relate to anyone, we must know which of their Brains is active and something about what that activity might be. And, in children, whose Brains are developing (and changing, based on the inputs we and the rest of the environment provide them), knowing what their Brains are up to is only possible if we understand — and are attuned to — what kind of Brains they are working with.

Medically, when nothing unusual happens during a pregnancy, and the mother is in a mentally happy state (with no fears about the pregnancy, her relationship, work, finances, her health, or her safety, and she is not using strong medication that regulates emotions (anti-depressants), there is a 99.9% chance that the baby is born with healthy, aligned Head, Heart and Gut Brains.

EXAMPLE: THE GRIEVING TWIN

I once saw a female client who had been a twin in the womb. In the third month of the pregnancy, her brother had died in the womb. When I met her, she was in her thirties, and she felt that she was always missing something in her life. She said that she was looking for "it" in every relationship, but never found this missing thing. It put a lot of pressure and expectation not only on her, but on her partner as well.

She once mentioned she feared that whenever she was in a relationship, her partner would leave her. So, in order to overcome this fear, she preferred keeping track of where her partner was and where he was going. In addition, she would constantly feel tired. She said she was always somehow missing her brother, even though she had other siblings.

We could say that her heart was still grieving, and logically she knew that but was unable to change it.

First, she really needed to heal her heart, the 'illogical' grief.

As this example shows, it is not always the case that a normal mental pregnancy results in the child's Three Brains being well aligned. This client's mother had had a normal pregnancy as far as she knew, except for this.

This kind of development is extremely important because children grow at an incredibly fast rate. A four-week-old fetus forms new neurons at a rate of 250,000 every minute. By the time a child is two, their brain will reach 80% of its adult volume and will process close to 1,500 billion connections between neurons. Up to the age of three, one million connections per second are made.[51] [52]

As a result of all that rapid brain development, 60% of a baby's metabolic energy, primarily the consumption of glucose, is spent on growing those soon-to-be massive Brains. In contrast, the brain of an adult uses only about 25% of the body's metabolic energy for the functioning of the Brains[53]. They just need sleep for that, and they can enjoy and live life in the moment, perfectly happy.

So, in these early years, most of the basic connections are installed for the Head, Heart and Gut Brains. Everything that happens will somehow influence the setup of our Brains, hence our decisions and actions are influenced by it.

The first two years of our life are extremely important for our later life.

17.

The first two years

In the first two years of our life, we are mostly in a state that is akin to deep hypnosis. (We call this a delta wave state.) Our Head Brain is working like a sponge. It absorbs everything it can: sounds, colors, words, and language.[54]

At this extremely busy time, our Gut Brain and other systems are also learning how to control our rapidly growing bodies. We learn gross motor control to move our arms and legs and then the fine controls required to manipulate things with our hands and to balance. Just imagine all the tiny adjustments you must make just to stand up and walk! No wonder a child falls down a thousand times before it has mastered the art of walking across a room. What this means in terms of Brain activity is this: In the first two years of our lives, we almost entirely live in this hyper-absorbent delta-wave state.[55]

During this time that the Head Brain is focused entirely on absorbing as much information as fast as it can, it is our Gut Brain and Heart Brain that are running the show. The Gut Brain, of course, is needed to be on task from the get-go. Its aim is to stay nourished, hydrated and rested. At the same time, your Heart Brain is trying to establish the emotional connections to the care givers that will help the Gut Brain get what it needs. It figures out who the caregivers are and bonds with them. Bonding has its own emotional rewards, so the Heart Brain responds to the care and tenderness it receives by learning to love those who supply those things.

Attachment

Until our second year of life, we are mostly in a delta brainwave pattern. Although this is deep sleep for adults, infants and very young children produce delta waves when they are conscious. They are downloading massive amounts of environmental data, soaking up the world through their five senses and recording and storing it in their subconscious mind for later use.[56] [57]

Based on that growth, we determine two things in the first two years of our life: whether there is a 'safe' or an 'unsafe' attachment.

Bessel van der Kolk, in his amazing book The body keeps the score,[58] writes about attachment theory. He explains that a lack of attachment, such as trust, safety and predictability with our parents or caregivers in the first two years of our life, can have a profound effect on us in later life.[59]

According to his research in America, he concludes that almost 40% of children have an insecure attachment with their parents.[60] This is a shocking statistic.

What we all deserve is a secure or safe attachment meaning that the children know and can trust what reaction the parent or caregiver will give in a particular situation. That means the reaction of the parent or caregiver is predictable and comes from a positive loving heart. This can still mean saying no to something, as long as it is from a positive caring attitude.

Take 'insecurity' as an example, in this story I heard from a client whose father was an alcoholic.

He said that he always listened with his sister when their father came home. They knew that if he was drunk, he would usually either hit them or their mother.

So, when he came home drunk, "we ran to our bedroom and hid. But the real horrendous thing was when we were wrong and thought he was sober but, in fact, he was drunk."

These traumatic experiences create an attachment on a different level with the father, mother, relationships and alcohol in future life: an insecure attachment.

When a parent at one moment gives their child a hug and at the next is shouting at them, it will create an insecure attachment because the toddler cannot predict what their mother, father or caregiver would do in that situation. They don't feel safe in the situation; the trust has been breached.

This happens more often when the parents or caregivers are dealing with a lot of their own issues, like financial instabilities, relationship issues like divorce, work or other conflicts. Of course, alcoholism or other addictions will result in imbalanced parenting.

If you are a parent and are now thinking that you are sometimes unpredictable in your response, don't worry! We are not talking here about occasional arguments, these will not severely traumatize your child for life. More is required for an insecure attachment to develop. Negative, unpredictable behavior from the parents needs to be present over a long period.

Nowadays, it happens more and more to children who are the collateral damage from a divorce. One or both of the parents may have developed a hatred towards the other and may talk negatively about the other parent, or are negative when the child says something positive about the other parent. As a result of this, those children may not feel safe with their parent anymore. They may not dare to share what they think or do and may create an unattached relationship with the parent.

Just imagine what kind of effect that could have when the little one is an adult and is engaging in a relationship. How much of a natural reflex do you think they will have to be totally open with their partner?

Bessel van der Kolk explains that toddlers have three strategies to deal with insecurities:[61]

- Avoiding attachment strategy, adopted by 37% of children.
- Anxious attachment strategy, adopted by 26% of children.
- Disorganized strategy, adopted by 37% of children.

When you read the explanation of these strategies, think about the people you know and see if you can recognize any of it in their current behavior.

'Avoiding' strategy. Observing children carrying out this behavior, on first: "It is like nothing is really bothering them, they are rather in-tuned". It looks as if they are okay with it when their mother is leaving. They show no behavior like crying, and when she returns, they act like they do not notice her. It is almost like they are ignoring her. So, from the outside view it is like everything is alright.

However, in the research study they also connected the little ones on a heart rate monitor, and on that moment the results of "everything is okay" became questionable. What the heart rate monitor showed is that the children have a chronically increased heart rate and it shows that they are in a constant state of "hyper-arousal".

The best way to describe their behavior is that they are "dealing but not connected with their feelings". This is a typical a Gut Brain response to protect the Heart Brain, it is shutting down the Heart Brain, probably you have experienced this feeling of having a closed heart. It is a normal thing to have experienced that after a painful breakup or betrayal but in this case, it is the default position for people

In this state the people do not show their emotions or what is bothering them; it looks like they are in a state of "cold" control and disconnection. Do any of your friends or colleagues come to mind?

What the studies revealed is that is that most mothers of avoidant infants touch their children less than other mothers. In the upbringing the little ones are less cuddled, they are less picked up for comfort and also hold their children less than other mothers. What is also observed in the studies is that they lack the use of facial expressions and their voice to create that synchronized connection.[62]

I think it is fair to conclude that these children are deprived from a real heart brain connection with their mother and therefore never learned how to open their heart so only trust their Gut Brain responses.

So how do you recognize these people. Imagine the people who can easily cut someone out of there life, hurt someone else without having regret or remorse. These people are in most cases the typical dominant Gut Brain people.

'Anxious' strategy. From the outside this behavior seems like the exact opposite of the avoided strategy. These children are much more expressive in their need to connect with their mother, they are crying, yelling, clinging, or screaming. This is happening when our Heart Brain that is asking for connection and the Gut Brain receives signals that the social safety is in danger. This activates the fear and/or angry responses to solve with this missing need. Although as we know it is not logical to do so these children have the belief that their actions will have a positive response.

What was also noticeable when their mother was leaving or when they did not know where she was, was that the children became enormously upset (Heart Brain becomes active as it feels abandoned). When she returned however and they became aware of this, they derived little comfort from this.

That makes dealing with people who suffer from this rather difficult as it is hard to comfort them. In the research it showed that paying them attention was not making them less upset because they did not believe or could not trust that this was genuine.

If we analyze this, we could almost conclude that they are in a state of constant fear/anger. They don't trust that help is going to stay if it is provided. Unless they make a spectacle to receive help, nobody is going to pay attention to them.

One of the other elements of the anxious strategy is that in situations when children are playing, they stay passively or angrily focused on their mother. We could say they want to have to be sure there is a connection and do not trust that it "normal" that the connection is there, but when it is there, they push it away as they still do not trust it is a genuine one. It seems they are "feeling but not dealing".[63]

It reminds me of a client couple I once saw. He told me that his partner always wanted to know where he was and what he was doing. He said he felt that even if he told her, it was never enough. She was always suspicious. It was almost impossible to satisfy her need of knowing or controlling.

'Disorganized' strategy. The third strategy is the most complicated one as here they are clueless what to do.

In the research study, when they observed such children, you can see them looking at their parents when they enter the room and then quickly turn away. It is like they are seeking closeness when they look at the parents and when they see then avoid them. What you could see in this situation that they rock on their hands and knees, or start glazing away like they go into a trance, or get up to go to their parent and then fall to the ground (This last one is an immobilization response of the Gut Brain).

We could draw the conclusion they are faced with an unsolvable dilemma: the need for connection and bonding with the parent for survival and on the same moment avoiding the parents as they have a sense that it is not safe. For some odd reason they are not able to use either strategy, not the anxious strategy (ask for attention) nor the avoiding strategy (shift attention or flee). This shows that the Gut Brain and Heart Brain are both active and pitifully are competing.

I would hypothesize that the anxious strategy is used by Heart Brain-dominant children who love to have connection, but their Gut Brain is pulling them back every time that the Heart Brain wants to connect.

In the avoiding strategy, the Gut Brain is activating the fight or flight response and the Heart Brain is turned off and becomes silent.

In the disorganized strategy, I would say all of the Brains are active, and when they take action, the Gut Brain activates the dorsal vagal nerve, which turns to a freeze or fold state. See The science behind our Three Brains to read more about this.

I would love for this to be researched so that we could find even more ways to help those children later in life.

These learned strategies can accompany us to our adulthood and the anxious toddlers become anxious adults, people who love to have connection but are afraid to trust that connecting is safe. The avoidant toddlers are likely to become adults who are disconnected with their own Heart Brain feelings and those of others.

Maybe you heard someone say, "There's nothing wrong with firm hand to steer. I got hit and it made me strong and the success I am today," or, "You cannot trust them so never share, they will use it against you," you can be sure this was an 'avoiding strategy' toddler, a traumatized Gut Brain person.

In school, avoidant children are more likely to become the bullies, while the anxious children are often their victims. When you think back to your school days. Can you put classmates' names to these two behaviors?

Whilst the disorganized toddlers have the greatest chance of becoming addicted or a client of the psychological health system.

However, the good thing is that development is not linear, and many life experiences can intervene to change these outcomes and undo, redo or alter these lessons learned in our early childhood. For more about this, go to the Section, Young people.

One of the conclusions of all of this research is that our need for attachment never reduces, we have that need to be connected. What makes sense as bonding and connection is the most important thing for babies to survive, it is almost hardwired.

It is intolerable for almost anybody to be disengaged from others for any length of time. Hence being sent back to your room as a kid or being put in isolation in jail is an immensely strong punishment. Nowadays this is why negative comments or being ghosted on social media have such a profound impact on people.

Social media thrives on this need to be connected and does everything to provide that feeling of bonding. Just think how you respond when you see a notification on your mobile phone, that someone liked your post or a friend is doing something? When we cannot connect through work, friendships or family, the reality is that many of us will create other, less positive ways of bonding, as examples, this can be through having an illness, a lawsuit or creating a conflict, as long as somehow, we can create the feeling that we have a connection.

Does this give you a clearer picture of partners, ex-partners, friends, or maybe family or colleagues?

What this means is that evolution hardwired us as social animals and created a Heart Brain with all the connecting emotions for that. When that's not fulfilled, we will use Gut survival or Head Brain manipulation strategies to achieve a connection.

18.

Ages two through five

After the age of about two, the balance begins to shift. To the people around us, it seems like we have 'woken up' to the world. For the next few years, until around the age of six, our Head Brains are still in something of a hypnotic state, but now use theta waves. In adults, theta brainwaves occur most often in sleep, and can also be elicited by deep meditation. A Brain in a theta wave state is open to learning and creating memories.

In a theta state, our senses are more attuned to signals originating from within, rather than focusing on external stimuli. So, when we note that the Head Brains of children are mostly in a theta brainwave state, it means that they are focused much more on trying to organize what their senses have already taken in, than on paying close attention to the world outside. To an adult who has already done this work, children at this age can seem dreamy and detached. When we try to force them to focus on new stimuli — like paying attention to what we are saying — they can react in unexpected (and sometimes unpleasant) ways.

Although at this age we are still absorbing new things at a tremendous rate, these are the years that the Head Brain also starts to act — we learn to read and write, and maybe ride a bike. Even so, our Head Brain is still a sponge — sucking new data out of every experience. How much information is getting filed away for later use? A kindergarten teacher put it to me this way: "I always have to remember that the day a new four-year-old walks through the door, he or she has already learned three-quarters of what they will ever know in their lives."

Even so, that remaining quarter is still an immense amount of information. In these years, by observing parents and siblings, we are learning how to socialize with family members and how our family system works. How do they communicate? How do they solve conflicts? What is the right thing to do when you are tired or hungry? How are things different in other situations, like at school or in the playground? Every observation is filed away in a storehouse of 'this is how it works' or 'best practices'.

At this stage of development, we are not able to rationalize or analyze — we mostly just parrot the behaviors we observe. In fact, we don't really have a grasp of the concept of time. To a kid at this age, 'next week' is a mythical land. The only thing that's real is 'now'. Popular psychology calls this the imprint period. It's a time when we believe in Santa Claus and fairy tales. After all, if we can cope with things that are purely imaginary, like 'next week', how much of a stretch is it, really, to throw Santa into the mix?

A common mistake parents make is thinking their **two- to six-year-old children** can **rationally discuss** their own actions. **They cannot.** This can be a huge frustration for the parents and children alike. The parent expects their kid to follow their logic and be, therefore, persuaded of something. Eventually, your kid may be worn down and will figure out what it is you want to hear. But it's not because you proved anything. Their Gut and Head Brains have just figured out the best, and safest, way to give you whatever you wanted. In short, you win nothing, and you've taught your kid one more way to outfox you.

Now just imagine how this learned behavior will be portrayed when that little one is an adult. They will know that they cannot win the argument even when they are right, and will just follow or disconnect; a bit of themselves is lost.

A more successful way to communicate with a child at that age is to communicate from the Gut and Heart Brains. Children can grasp a structure and they can follow rules — whether they follow the logic behind them or not. Yes/No. Right/Wrong. Good/Bad. Safe/Dangerous. These are all things that a kid can understand. So, in these years, you educate their Gut and Heart Brains by letting them know what works for their world and yours, and what does not. Years later, they will understand the thinking. In these years, they can only take in what works and what does not.

This means we communicate to children at this stage that the most important thing for them to understand is that they are safe, and that they are loved; that following certain guidelines will help keep them safe and that those guidelines are not negotiable.

ANECDOTE: RULES ARE NOT MADE TO BE BROKEN

Once, at a friend's house, I witnessed exactly how rules can crumble under pressure. My friend's five-year-old was testing to see if a rule was real.

At 7:00 pm, the parents said it was bedtime. First, the child made a case that he should be allowed another half hour to finish what he was doing. To avoid having a conflict in front of a guest, the parents gave in.

Afterward, when the kid had finally gone to bed, he came out, asking for a cookie and milk. He was told no and send back to bed with a sad face and some tears. But that was not the end of it. The child reappeared again and again. Each time, the parents held to the rule. Bedtime means Bedtime. Somewhere around nine, when the kid asked for the sixth or seventh time, they caved: "Okay, just this once, take a cookie, drink your milk and then go to bed."

So, what did Junior's hyper-absorbent Gut Brain and Head Brain take from this? "If I keep asking, the rule will go away". Or, more accurately, "There is no rule."

[We will see how this dynamic turned out for both parents and child in the chapter Teenagers. Spoiler alert: Not well.]

As we know from earlier discussions, a Gut Brain cannot learn when it does not feel safe. This is the time in which a person's fundamental attitude toward life and other people is formed. Changing that attitude in later years can be very difficult. In fact, depending on the power of the experiences that create a person's attitude, it can be close to impossible to re-school such bedrock beliefs.

At this age, the foundation is laid for self-esteem, self-worth and self-confidence.

The theory of Transactional Analysis explains this by the four approaches to life that we create, based on the four ways we communicate and educate our children:

- **I'm OK and You're OK:** This is the healthiest position about life. A person with this attitude feels good about themselves and about others. They are inclined to trust both the intentions and the competence of others. There is a willingness to give and take, and an acceptance of others as they are. People are close to themselves and to others. There are no losers, only winners. In my words a healthy Heart and Gut Brain, the Gut Brain feels safe and the Heart Brain feels good about themselves.

- **I'm OK and You're Not OK:** A person with this attitude feels good about themselves, but views others with suspicion. They project their problems onto others and blame them, put them down, and criticize them. They view others as damaged, incompetent and untrustworthy. This position is that of the person who needs an underdog to maintain his or her sense of 'OK-ness'. Here the Gut Brain is alert and does not have a safe feeling as the basis hence it puts the other down. The Heart Brain has scars from the past therefore it does not trust the other person.

- **I'm Not OK and You're OK:** A person with this attitude sees themselves as damaged goods and feel powerless (depressed) in a world populated by people who are better than they are. They are inclined to accept the position of being the weak partner in a relationship — as others in life are more competent and better people. The person who approaches life in this way is an easy target for manipulation or abuse, as typically such people serve others' needs instead of their own. Here the Gut Brain is just like the previous position alert and isn't feeling safe. Furthermore, it does not have the self-confidence to win so it acts submissively. The Heart Brain also has scars from the past from having experienced it is not good enough.

- **I'm Not OK and You're Not OK:** This is the most troublesome approach to life of all. People who approach life in this way believe that the entire world, themselves included, are foolish, incompetent, and immoral. They are inclined to be angry, isolated, depressed, and hopeless. Rebuilding from this state is possible, but it requires patience and a great deal of hard work. Unfortunately, people who feel this way about the world are the least likely to seek, or to accept, the help they need to change their approach. Here the Gut Brain is just like the previous positions alert and does not have a safe feeling. It does not have the self-confidence to win so it escapes the situation and behaves as a loner. The Heart Brain also has scars from the past from having experienced it is not good enough.

With children especially, we need to make sure that we interact with them in the first of these styles. They need to know that they are loved unconditionally. Why? Because a child's Head Brain is a sponge that, at this stage of development, has no understanding that the experiences of others could be different from its own. It believes that what it observes of the world is the way things are for everyone, and it encodes in its Gut Brain the rules of behavior based on its own experience. In this kind of communication, we create a healthy Gut Brain that feels safe and a Heart Brain that feels loved, hence self-esteem, self-worth and self-confidence.

So, what's wrong with "I love you because..." or, "If you loved me, you would..."? The Gut Brain and Heart Brain learn by such conditional positive statements that they are loved, not for themselves, but because they have met some qualification test — some condition. A child who grows up feeling that the love they need can be withdrawn if they fail to meet their caregiver's criteria, is a child whose Gut Brain will be constantly on the alert. However good their intentions, a parent or caregiver who uses fear, obligation, or guilt to educate the child is baking anxiety, and perfectionism, into the core of their personality.

WHAT DOES THIS SOUND LIKE IN REAL LIFE?

"I worked hard on that dinner. If you loved me, you would eat it."

"I had a hard day today, so be a good boy and put the garbage outside."

"I cooked dinner, so be a good girl and clean the kitchen."

"A good kid knows where their place is."

"When you have a 9 or higher on your test, you are great."

"You can only be successful and be like me when you suffer pain and hardship."

"I hit/punish you because I love you and want you to be a good adult."

"A good girl serves her man."

"A real boy does not cry."

Although such interactions are meant to educate a child about proper behavior, the lesson the Gut Brain learns is not the one intended. Rather than learning to make mature decisions, the Gut Brain and Heart Brain learn that it's best to give way to authority — even if it doesn't understand why. To be loved, you have to do something.

Even worse would be the conditional negative version: "Eat the food I cooked for you or I'll make you regret it." That simply adds fear, a sure-fire way to make a child feel unsafe and, therefore, opening the door to Gut Brain hyper-vigilance — otherwise known as insecurity and anxiety.

So, when we 'survive' our early childhood without too much damage, or in most cases, luckily, have happy, positive memories, we start our school career. There we may unfortunately become aware of the 'rules' of some schoolmates and teachers: bullying, abuse and stereotyping.

19.

The pre-teen years, from two to Three Brains

Where the first six years are called the 'imprint period', the time to our 14th year is called the 'modeling period'; we model the world, school, friends, teachers, and our parents.

At around the age of six, we become less susceptible to outside programming, with the increasing appearance of higher frequency alpha waves. Alpha activity is equated with states of calm, conscious awareness. While most of our senses — such as sight, hearing, and smell — observe the outer world, consciousness is kind of a 'sense organ' that mirrors the inner workings of the body's own cellular community. It is an awareness of 'self'. We start really developing a sense of individual personhood — separate from those around us — and all Three Brains get activated.

Brainwave development shows that your child will also now establish an alpha state, that zone when we are just relaxed as an adult but where children are in an extreme state of learning.

Alpha is 'the power of now', being here, in the present. Alpha is the resting state for the brain. Alpha waves aid overall mental coordination, calmness, alertness, mind/body integration and learning. Alpha activity has also been connected to the ability to recall memories, lessened discomfort and pain, and reductions in stress and anxiety. For kids, entering this alpha wave state means that the Head Brain is one step closer to fully functioning.

This is the moment when our Head Brains really develop that sense of 'Me' and 'Us', and past, present and future. This is also the time when we really start seeing differences in people. We can see the manifestation of their upbringing in the previous years, how they judge and behave with others, how safe they feel, and how much they think, "I'm OK and you're ok".

This is the time that we start thinking logically. Most children develop a sense of time in this period. By age nine, the future becomes much more real. 'Next week' is no longer a myth, it will be here soon. 'Next month' is not very far off. And, finally, a child begins to process the idea that the things they do now can influence what happens later.

At this stage of development, the Head Brain comes out of its hyper-absorption phase and begins to contribute to a child's decision-making process.

So, are we, at the age of nine, fully functional decision-making machines, with balanced and fully formed Brains, each playing their life-long roles in our personalities and decision making? As if, we are just halfway, maybe two-thirds at best!

The first 18 years of development are extremely important for a child, and in this pre-teen period, we still can have a hugely positive (and negative) influence as a parent.

I think everybody who has children knows that our impact as parents greatly diminishes the moment they hit secondary school (high school).

During those precious years between 9 and 13, your child can still be that little one who likes to sit on your lap one moment, and say later when you give them a cuddle, "Mommy/Daddy, don't be so stupid." As their Head Brain starts developing its rational part, the learning role of the Gut Brain and the Heart Brain becomes less.

This is the time when they really start understanding the explanations that you give them. Now they start understanding why it is not nice to hit their brother.

This is the time when your example behavior as parents becomes extremely important, because you can explain your behavior to them.

Explain to them why you/they did something "good" or "not so smart", and you can correct the learning in their brain when you, as a parent, do something "not so smart".

Whereas, before this age, they took everything you did for granted, and your 'example' behavior was the only right route to take and adopt, now it can be challenged and moderated.

Now they start to understand when you come home tired and are less sociable, because your Gut Brain needs to have a little rest.

At this time, your role as parent is changing from just showing example behavior to also explaining why it is example behavior and why it is sometimes not.

This is a beautiful time, as you can still turn some switches in your child's development, because they're still willing to listen to you.

In the Waldorf schooling system[64]–this system is based on the educational philosophy of Rudolf Steiner, the founder of anthroposophy, it strives to develop pupils' intellectual, artistic, and practical skills in an integrated and holistic manner, focusing particularly on the cultivation of pupils' imagination and creativity, this age is also when they really start teaching children things that are based on Head Brain learning. In the preceding years, all the learning is done by playing and socializing, i.e. a focus on teaching the Gut and Heart Brains.

20.

Teenagers, Three Brains
struggling for control

O k, so you (and your kid) have survived your child's pre-teen years, those crucial formative and modeling years when Brains are forming and learning about the world and about how to fit into a family and a community. So, it's got to be smooth sailing from here, right?

Anyone who's lived with a teenager under their roof knows the adventure is just beginning. Sometimes the idea that your teenager has a brain at all will seem to exceed even the most accommodating of adults' Heart Brain's capacity for optimism. Teens have, of course, the same three that other humans have. But how they function and how they interact is profoundly different from when they were younger, and nowhere close to what they will be like when they become adults.

At 12 years old, a child's EEG spectrum begins to show sustained periods of high-frequency beta brainwaves. Beta brain states are characterized as 'active or focused consciousness', Now, finally, they really start fully using their Head Brains.

It does not mean they are wise. At this stage, children will start developing their independence, learning how to stand on their own two feet.

If a child feels safe and secure in their first 12 years, they will live in a world of happy and hopeful possibilities. They will look to the future optimistically. They will believe in their own strengths. If, on the other hand, a child at this age is insecurely attached, their Gut Brain and Heart Brain will be out of sync with one another. The Heart Brain may yearn for connections — but the Gut Brain will be afraid and may shy away from them.

From now on, their brainwaves look like those of an adult brain. The beta and gamma brainwaves are there. Also, their Head Brain's self-awareness has come into full bloom. They know who they are — and are independent of those around them.

They can understand and have opinions about what is happening around them. They start being able to make decisions about life, based on an understanding of what can happen in the future. The Heart Brain and Gut Brain now start incorporating the Head Brain's analysis and predictions into their decision-making process.

As they wrestle, internally, with the decisions they are making about their actions, their lives and their futures, they find themselves as often in conflict with their parents as with themselves. The Gut Brain wants to make decisions that are independent of external controls and lets the Heart and Head Brains know that it's time to start thinking for themselves. It is important to note here that this balance and brain development is constantly changing. Our Head Brains only become fully developed in girls between 16 and 18 and in boys a couple of years later, between 18 and 21.

Communication with your teen's Brains is much more complicated than it was before, which is one reason why it is imperative to keep the lines of understanding and communication open. We may miss the time in which our children's Brains were, essentially, molding themselves to conform with our own approach to life, but those years are gone, and nothing we can do or say will bring them back. The teenage years are the ones in which parents need to adjust to the fact that their precious young ones are now real people. For these next few teenage years however, the love and trust that were established in the younger years will pay off. That connection can help us to continue to communicate with our teenager's Brains. And it could not be more important that we do. This is the time that real-life dangers are omnipresent and real-life consequences have become very real indeed.

As independent as they may feel or yearn to be, they do still need us. Unfortunately, these are also the years in which the Gut Brain's desire for independence can interrupt its compulsion to keep us safe. Torn as they are, teenage Gut Brains become very bad at calculating odds. As a result, teenagers take risks that boggle the minds of the adults in their lives.

Inexperienced teenage Gut Brains are often deluded into thinking that amongst the things from which they can assert independence are the laws of physics and probability. Yes, even survival-focused Gut Brains can believe they are along for a thrilling ride as an immortal being.

Risk-taking is a risk for teenagers

So what decisions are our teenagers' Three Brains making that allow them to take extraordinary risks? And how can we educate those Brains without taking away all the thrill of being young, healthy and alive?

You can't of course, talk to hormones. But you can, and should, try to educate the Brain that releases them. Here are some ways to do that:

Having a properly developed Gut Brain is essential for girls and boys to get safely through their teenage years. While the Head Brain is fully present, it is not fully developed. Neither teens themselves, nor their parents, can fully trust the Head Brain's partially informed decision-making process. That will be honed by years of trial, error, feedback, correction and (hopefully) different errors. In that time, a trusted parent, teacher or caregiver can, and should, play an important part in the feedback and correction part of the learning process — but it must be done carefully and supportively, or the Gut Brain will sense danger and shut off that channel of communication.

So, in practical terms, what does that leave us with? While we are helping a teenager's Head Brain to learn the ropes of mature, rational decision-making, it will be the fully developed Gut Brain that we must engage to keep our teens from going off the rails. Having a discussion with them about this is bound to be challenging. But it is our lifeline in these years. And it can be done.

How to defang a teenager's Gut Brain

As we all know by now, the first step when you engage anyone's Gut Brain is to create safety. Remember that any interaction a teenager has with a parent or authority figure will be treated as a threat until proven otherwise. As a result, almost every interaction you have with a teen is going to start with a Gut Brain reaction, most commonly avoid, divert or flee. If you let your own Gut Brain take charge of the interaction, the encounter is likely to start badly and get worse.

The main thing a teenager needs to know and feel is that he or she is safe — in other words, what he or she is doing is not being judged. This does not mean you cannot disagree with the actions. But anything that sounds like a judgment will be interpreted as a threat.

So how does this work? How do you get past the watchdog to have a meaningful and productive discussion? Let's think back to our trigger words.

If what comes out of your mouth is something that sounds like a criticism, for example, "What were you thinking?" or, "That was a stupid thing to do," your teenager's Gut Brain will fully engage.

On the other hand, "I disagree with what you're doing" is a way to bring their Head Brain into the discussion. If you want to engage the Heart Brain, then you might focus on the affection and attachment you have to each other, and then put the decision you would want to be reconsidered in the context of that relationship.

As the parent, you are still the authority figure. You still are a person who can set boundaries and rules. The question here is how you do that, and to which Brain you communicate those boundaries and rules. If it's the Gut Brain, you will find yourself fighting (and sometimes losing) many battles that didn't have to happen.

Firstly, your teenager should know and feel that you love them unconditionally. Secondly, you should create a safe place so the Gut Brain can go into the background and you can have a discussion with the more thoughtful and considerate Brains that your teen has (even if it seems you don't often hear from them, make no mistake, they are there). And, yes, this is for you to accomplish; your Brains are more developed and, one hopes, more capable of regulating one another than those of your teenager.

One of the golden rules to be able to have that discussion is to really understand your teenager's needs. What is he or she trying to achieve? You were once a teenager, after all. So, when you can channel your inner teen and understand what he or she wants or needs, then you can start having a discussion, because you have (clever you!) moved the discussion away from judgment and onto the turf of wants, needs and desires. Many a bad — and seemingly incomprehensibly foolish — decision is rooted in a (if misguided or immature) desire to accomplish something worthwhile (or, at least, understandable) **and that is their decision, not yours**. A desire to be seen as interesting, to be popular, to connect to a social group — these are the things that drive most teenage decisions away from connecting to you as caregiver, to connecting to others as they are their future.

The moment you can shift the discussion from actions/behavior to the needs they are trying to fulfill, the tone of the talk will be totally different. And you may have a chance to impart some real wisdom into the bargain. Maybe the people your teen is seeking to appeal to are not the ones he or she truly wants to be like. Maybe the fear of rejection is causing real anguish. These are things you would never learn, if the encounter began and ended with Gut Brain combat.

Examples of how to provide feedback and guidance to a Head Brain's trial and error process

The saying "you reap what you sow" applies to 95% of the time when we are raising children. When in the early development of children, you educate them with proper boundaries and, even more importantly, with clear boundaries that are not negotiable (Yes = Yes and No = No), what you will reap in their teenage years is someone much more attuned to holding themselves back from excessively risky behavior. Actually, your decisions are seen as their own independent decisions!

As we discussed in early childhood years, the Gut and Heart Brains are sponges. They absorb everything as true, without rationalizing or understanding. If the boundaries or rules are constantly changing, the lesson learned is that there are no real rules. When that is what happened in the early years, then a teen has nothing they know to be true to fall back on when faced with a decision.

To be extremely blunt, the Gut and Heart Brains have similar qualities to the brain of a cat or a dog, so it makes sense to educate those Brains in a similar way. Our Heart Brain doesn't have the logical, analytical capacities of the Head Brain, and the Head Brain is only fully part of the cerebral mix after a child turns 12. In essence, the boundaries and rules you set for a child when he or she is younger will be those that guide your teenager internally, at a time when it is close to impossible to communicate with the independence-oriented teenage Brains that are not interested in what you have to say.

Remember that kid who got his parents to break the 'Bedtime means Bedtime' rule? When he was 14, his parents asked me if I could work with him. He had grown rebellious. He would not listen to his parents; he always went for the 'battle' and most of the time it ended in a 'verbal fight'.

21.

Children and divorce, consistency and honesty is the key

With a divorce rate now of 50% in the Western world, raising children to live with two sets of rules is increasingly common — and is a problem that must be addressed. When parents' divorce and go their separate ways, the children are likely to be bouncing back and forth between parents with two different styles of educating and rule-setting. (Sometimes this is already established, as the issue of differing styles is often one of the reasons parents decide they can't live together.)

One true prescription for problems is when parents get into competition with one another for a child's respect or affection.

Maintaining rules and boundaries is hard work. And no parent wants to be the 'hard asses. So, rules are relaxed. Sometimes, they are relaxed by a parent who has their child only on weekends. Weekends are not school nights, after all. Other times, the school-night parent is overwhelmed, overworked or just pressed for time. Either way, children end up insecurely attached to both, since there is no consistency to the information their Brains are absorbing about how the world works.

Parents who have to compete on the field of gratifying desires can really set the stage for a confusing and inconsistent world for their children. The entire balance is upended when one parent buys the child an iPad, the other parent a game console, then both try to use those purchases to curry favor. Children quickly learn to manipulate situations like this to get lots of great stuff. But their developing Gut and Heart Brains are learning that the love they are feeling is conditional, transactional and unreliable.

How can we now think it strange that many young people today seem dismissive of authority or of limits on their behavior? Their internal limits are as flexible as the ones they were raised with.

When I work with young adults who experienced this, they often say things like, "I will only have children when I know 100% the relationship will last." This would be a positive statement, if it were based on their learnings and not a response to the divorce trauma they have experienced.

A lot of clients ask me, especially when they are facing a divorce, or have already gone through a divorce, "Can we protect our children from the damage of our divorce?" and, "Can we undo the horrible things that happened before the divorce?" The last question comes to me a lot when one of the parents is abusive/addictive/did not solve his/her own issues and projected them onto the children or partner.

As a real optimist, I would say yes. Although a lot of wiring and pathways have been established in the Gut and Heart Brains, we can do amazing stuff as parents and change the routing of those pathways/wiring.

It means we really have to turn to unconditional positive/love communication and use a lot of explanations about why we do what we do, and the difference between our intentions and the actual behavior we express.

The reason unconditional positive/love communication is key in this change, is because it provides safety for the Gut Brain. That allows the Gut Brain to open the gateways to learning, because it turns off the fight or flight response and the immobilization response.

Hence the Gut Brain, the Heart Brain, and the Head Brain can then fully function, learn and reroute the wiring.

I will not say it is easy, because it means we need to show consistent, congruent behavior ourselves, and the capacity to reflect on our own behavior, to explain why we did what we did and why it was good/bad, constructive/non constructive, intentional vs real behavior and the capacity to say sorry, etc.

There are enough examples of orphans who came from an orphanage to a foster family, and who turned out to be amazing adults. This is rerouting of wiring in action.

The flip-side of the coin is if we don't, we program our children to follow this example in how to see the world and relationships.

Where it goes wrong after divorce so many times is that we as the divorced parents are so extremely busy getting our own lives back on track, that we 'forget' our example behavior.

I have heard and seen too many examples where one of the parents is using the children in the 'battle' with the ex, by telling the children all the negative things the other parent did, withdrawing them from seeing the other parent, or not showing up for agreed custody arrangements.

The moment you start being negative about their other parent, you activate the child's Gut Brain, because it 'thinks' it's not safe to say nice things about the other parent. In addition, you create a huge loyalty conflict in the Heart Brain. The Heart Brain loves to love Mommy and Daddy, and then they are told not to love but to hate. And not because the parent is doing something horrendous to them, but because the parent broke up with the other parent and are educating their child to fight their war.

Their Head Brain does all it can to understand this concept of loving somebody, yet not be allowed to love that person because if you do so you show disloyalty to the other parent, and tries to explain it to the Heart Brain. In most cases it has little success, because how can you logically explain something like this?

This could create issues with their own relationships later in life, as they are taught not to trust their Heart Brain/Head Brain in a relationship. They did not learn how to match up real information they are feeling and observing by themselves and the information they got from the 'hateful' parent. A lot of those adults will have issues with fully opening their heart, because there will always be a little voice from their Gut Brain that tells them either they or their partner is not lovable, or that their partner doesn't love them and they should hate them.

When we summarize connecting with children after a divorce, it is all about being aware of the primary domination of the Gut Brain/Heart Brain in their learning process; their Head Brain doesn't start understanding the world until they reach 12 years old.

Section 6:

FOR ALL THE NERDIES LIKE ME, THREE BRAIN SCIENCE

These days, most of the research is still focused on the Head Brain. We are just beginning to understand how our Brains interact. As we learn more, our ability to apply that knowledge to heal people will grow by leaps and bounds.

We all know what it feels like to have our hearts broken. We have all experienced a gut feeling that doesn't seem logical — but we understand it to be true.

22.

The science behind our Three Brains

Let's start with the medical proof of why the Heart and the Gut are actually Brains, and why are they so crucial in understanding your partner. Once this fact is established, we will then discuss how they communicate.

It was not so long ago that Western medical science proved what we already knew (but without proof) about our amazing heart. It can be broken, and it can be hurt; because it can store memories of all the good and bad experiences we have had. It influences the Head and Gut Brains and it has a voice of its own.

Scientific proof of the Three Brains

Back in 1991, neurocardiology researcher, Dr J Andrew Armour, of the University of Montreal, introduced the concept of a functional Heart Brain.[65]

In his ground-breaking research work in the field of neurocardiology, he established that the heart is a sensory organ and a sophisticated information-encoding and processing center, with an extensive, intrinsic nervous system, sufficiently sophisticated enough to qualify as a 'Heart Brain'.

He researched and analyzed that the heart has on average 90,000 neurons, similar to those found in some areas of the brain.

The interesting fact is that research revealed that there is actually a huge variation in the number of brain cells somewhere between 40,000 and 120,000 brain cells. People who have a more social life and live life more from a positive attitude were found to have up to 120.000 Brains cells in the heart and people who lived a more isolated and depressed life came close to 40.000 brain cells in the heart.

Scientific evidence has shown that the heart sends emotional and intuitive information signals to the brain and body, and that it can learn, remember, feel, and sense.

Even more interesting our heart brain produces the hormones oxytocin (also known as the love hormone which is involved in cognition, tolerance, trust, friendship and the establishment of enduring pair-bonds), dopamine (the famous reward and motivation hormone) and norepinephrine (general function is to mobilize the brain and body for action)[66] [67]

Interestingly, he found out that the heart sends more information to the Head Brain than the Head Brain does to the heart.

The proof that the heart can remember is often seen in heart transplants. The amazing thing is that 10-15% of heart donation recipients experience changes in their tastes, personalities, and memories, picking up on information about the heart's original owner which was stored in the heart itself. This is attributed to functional cell memory.[68]

It has also been proven that the heart communicates with the brain and body in four different ways, creating the heart–brain feedback mechanism:

- Neurological communication of the nervous system by the vagus nerve in both afferent and efferent loops.
- Biochemical communication with hormones produced in the heart, traveling in our bloodstream to signal body and brain.[69]

- Biophysical communication through pulse waves–every time the heart beats, it creates pulse waves of pressure that are sensed by the body and brain. They are similar to sound waves in terms of their information-carrying capacity.
- Energetic communication using electromagnetic energy which travels through the body and brain. Amazingly, the heart generates a magnetic field which is 5,000 times more powerful than that of the brain. It can be measured from more than nine meters away from the body.[70] [71] [72]

It seems surprising that Western medical science didn't discover that the heart works as a brain until 1991. It had, in fact already been described in this way, 150 years earlier, but the idea had never really been taken seriously by medical science.

In 1865, Claude Bernard, a French physiologist, wrote, "In man the heart is not only the central organ of circulation of blood, it is a center influenced by all sensory influences. They may be transmitted from the periphery through the spinal cord, from the organs through the sympathetic nervous system, or from the central nervous system itself. In fact, the sensory stimuli coming from the brain exhibit their strongest effects on the heart."[73]

In 1872, Charles Darwin acknowledged and wrote about the dynamic neural relationship between the heart and the brain:[74]

> "…when the heart is affected and emotions are arising it influences the brain and the facial expressions and the brain communicates back to the heart via the vagus nerve on the heart; these two important organs are in a constant action and reaction."

So, it wasn't really a new discovery in 1991, it was more a rediscovery and a rather important one, because now finally medical science is accepting as fact that the heart remembers, thinks, and communicates to the Head Brain.

When we try to swallow this idea, it is essential to describe the other Brain, our Gut Brain. We all know and use the expression, "I have a gut feeling" or, "I cannot stomach that." Despite speaking about our other Brains, it still took until 1998 for it to be describes as a fact, when neurobiologist, Dr Michael Gershon, published his pivotal book, The Second Brain. In this book, he described his findings based on decades of research, during which he discovered that the gut contains a complex and fully functional neural network; what we could call a 'Brain'.[75]

The Gut Brain is officially called the intricate system and has about the same number of neurons and white matter as a cat's brain.

This means that there are approximately 500 million neurons active in our gut.

Furthermore, research has shown that the Gut Brain can learn, store memories, and perform complex independent processes.

It might even be more important to us than the Head Brain, as the Gut Brain is in charge of producing many hormones which regulate the body's emotions and mental wellbeing. As an example, it produces more then 90% of the serotonin in the body, therefore is a primary natural medicine factory and warehouse for feel-good hormones.[76]

It is often believed that the limbic brain (part of the Head Brain) is responsible for the production of hormones and especially the amygdala, but it is actually the Gut Brain (enteric brain) which is the main factory of the production and release of the neurotransmitter's serotonin, dopamine, glutamate, norepinephrine, and nitric oxide. Moreover, 70% of your immune system is in the gut.[77]

Interestingly, Head Brain diseases like Alzheimer's and Parkinson's often arise due to gut issues like constipation.[78] [79] More surprising is that issues like constipation take place due to the damage done on the neurons in the Brains, as occurring in the cranial brain (Head Brain).

Last but not least, peptides and endorphins have also been found in the gut.

What I love to tell my clients and patients who are addicted to antidepressants is that their gut is the best drug dealer in the world. It is a large provider of benzodiazepines, which are the psychoactive chemicals used in popular drugs, such as Valium and Xanax.

Michael Gershon's research showed that in times of massive acute stress, the gut produces enough benzodiazepines to calm and sedate the Head Brain. In much larger quantities it can be supplied by our own Gut Brain factory in those moments which results in the down-regulation of the cognitive and emotional stress response.

Our Gut Brain literally shuts down the Head Brain, so it does not freak out too much. It is as if your Gut Brain is telling your Head Brain, "You are not capable of dealing with this; I'll take care of it all."

You might have had the experience of getting choked from being emotional.

This happens when the Gut Brain regulates the muscles in the esophagus (the part of the alimentary canal which connects the throat to the stomach) and can stop us from swallowing food during times of danger and high stress. Even if we want to, we can't eat or swallow.

According to Gershon, as much as 90% of the communication between these two Brains goes from our gut to our brain.[80]

In other words, for every signal/command from the brain to the gut, nine signals' commands are sent to the brain from the gut.

And, last but not least, of course we have the remarkable brain in our head, the most capable out of all the three.

Although I refer to that as one brain, it is a combination of three separate ones. This is because it is beautifully constructed following three evolutionary layers.

The oldest one is commonly called the 'reptilian brain'. This is actually not true as even reptilians have the same genetic brain setup as mammals, meaning that they the DNA setup to have a limbic and neocortex[81] This brain is overlooking and controlling the body's vital functions such as heart rate, breathing, body temperature and balance. This part of our brain includes the brainstem and the cerebellum, the connection with the Gut Brain.

The limbic brain is developed as a center where all the information of feelings, emotions, social activities, and relationships come together. The primary structures of the limbic brain are the hippocampus, the amygdala, and the hypothalamus, it has a direct connection with the Heart and Gut Brain.

The neocortex brain controls thinking, memory, and regulation of impulses, and resides in the human brain with its two large cerebral hemispheres that play such a dominant role. These hemispheres are responsible for the development of human language, abstract thought, imagination and consciousness. The neocortex is flexible and has almost infinite learning abilities. This brain is also what has enabled us as humans to develop to where we are now.

When I talk about our Head Brain, I'm referring mostly to the primate neocortex brain.

So how come the Heart and Gut Brains were scientifically discovered more than a century ago, yet it has taken up to now to find about them?

That's because all the research that has been conducted for the last 100 years is based on how our Head Brain functions, and how these three layers are interacting with each other. Psychology considers only the head and dismisses the body as a neural center. Also, western medical science disconnects the Head from the Body when illnesses are researched.

From 2013 to 2016, I experimented with the idea of our Three Brains. I started to post videos about it on YouTube, after I learned in 2011 from Robert Dilts about his somatic work. I then learned more about the trauma work from Peter Levine and his amazing insights into how the body remembers and is actually in charge. In 2016, I received a text message from a fellow NLP teacher, who enlightened me with the fact that Grant Soosalu and Marvin Oka had already written a book about the Three Brains, using your multiple Brains to do cool stuff, in 2012.[82] I was happy and surprised that I was on the right track. Although we share our ideas about this brain theory, Soosalu and Oka have slightly different views on what these Brains do or are responsible for and much more importantly on the hierarchy of decision making. The main principles of having Three Brains are the same however. I would have loved to discuss with Grant about his and my ideas and put our Brains and insights together but sadly he died in 2019 at the time I was writing the previous edition of this book.

Evolution of our Three Brains

In order to understand why the Gut Brain is the actual Brain that decides if and when the other Brains are allowed to collaborate, it is good to dive into the strange world of evolution.

Let's take a look at how evolution made it from one little cell to 37 trillion cells (although other research suggests we are made up of 100 trillion cells), and why it created the Three Brains instead of one,

By the way if you think that is a lot, an octopus has 9 different Brains.

When you ponder your existence, do you ever think about exactly what we are? To answer that question biologically, we are 37 trillion cells all working together in beautiful harmony in order to exist. To make it easier, I'm not including the 100 trillion alien cells we have inside our bodies; without those bacteria inside us, we would die within a day. We have about one and a half kilograms of bacteria in our gut, and those are all essential for digesting our food; without those, there is no digestion and, therefore, no life.

Research shows that an imbalance of these alien cells in our body can create serious diseases. Nowadays, there is a hypothesis that the gluten and sugars we eat contribute to conditions like autism, stress, obesity, and more, because they create inflammation in our gut and alter the population of the gut bacteria. In order to understand why the human body has to depend on other life forms to literally exist, we need to go back further in time. Are you ready for a two-minute evolution ride?

It all started one billion years ago with a unicellular organism, a cell that consumed food and excreted waste material, as they still do now.

When cells started to work together, they turned into, let's say, 'living creatures' (multicellular organisms). It became a bit more complicated to consume food, digest, and reproduce. If every cell did that, the system could not work, so the cells started to mutate and to specialize. In a multicellular organism, the different cells work together for greater efficiency. Just like individuals in a team, every cell has its own purpose and functionality. Some became skin cells, some became muscle cells, some became intestine cells, some became reproduction cells, and so on.

One of the 'simple' examples of a multicellular organism is a sea cucumber. It ideally represents an early stage of evolution.

When you picture a sea cucumber, and we are making incredibly black-and-white comparisons here, does it not share many similarities with our digestive system?

A sea cucumber has a mouth, a stomach, intestines, and an exit, the anus. So, when it wants to process food through its body, it actually needs to think about digesting it. That is what the human gut does.

If this sea cucumber were placed in your body, it would make sense to say that there would be an individual brain in your gut.

Later, fish came to this world, as did the reptiles, and a more complex nervous system was required to operate the fins and other body parts. The spine evolved to protect the central nervous system and worked as the communication pathway to the different organs and ligaments.

All of these creatures — the sea cucumber, reptiles and fish — have something in common: they're all cold-blooded and do not possess a 4-chamber heart and therefore a brain as we humans have.

This means that the temperature of their bodies does not stay at a certain level. We can see that in reptiles; they must bask under the sunlight to raise their body temperature.

The warm-blooded mammals came to this world 400 million years ago and introduced the lifestyle of living in social groups, and let's not forget the birds that also created social groups like Crows. New conditioning was required, resulting in the growth and further evolution of the heart brain, which became more important as an additional Brain. Besides that, the limbic part of our Head Brain became more important to deal with the extra information it had to process in living in social groups.

Similarly, for humans, 1 to 2.5 million years ago, the neocortex of the human brain, as we know it, became a part of us. Before that, we had a tiny neocortex. We can see this in our domestic cats or dogs; they have a neocortex layer which is quite small when compared to a human brain.

Although we have similarities with primates, we have also one major difference that makes us human.

Tetsuro Matsuzawa is a Japanese Professor for Advanced Study of the Primate Research Institute, at Kyoto University. He tells us that the predecessors of the chimpanzees and humans lived in the forest and for some odd reason, our ancestors moved to live in the open fields. That is when humans needed to learn to communicate in a better way. To survive in their new environment, language was essential, as was learning from past experiences and predicting the future. This is called the 'Cognitive Trade-off Hypothesis'. Humans lost their extreme short-term memory, which chimpanzees still have. Humans learned the gift of language and developed a more time-related memory. Therefore, the brain became much more significant than it had been and more brain power and capacity was needed; hence the development of our human neocortex.[83]

What is the main difference between an animal's concept of time and consciousness, and that of humans? Just observe your pet, and you will see they do not remember yesterday, nor have any worries about tomorrow. Animals always live in the present; they do not understand what is going to happen next week or what happened last week. I have to say that makes me sometimes jealous as they forget all the bad things from the past. Our pets do not have ulcers from stress.

Learning from the past and planning for the future is an excellent benefit for survival, and that is one of the primary functions of the neocortex: remembering. Our Head Brain is like one big database of memories and experiences of the past, with the capacity and capability of making predictions for the future.

So, returning to our previous question, if we knew this, why did it take so long to discover the connection between the Three Brains? The answer is simple: in Western society, we have separated the brain from the body. We have psychologists, counsellors, and other professionals who work with mental illnesses, and we have medical practitioners who have their own specialties, such as cardiology, gastroenterology, orthopedics, and around 70 more (according to Wikipedia, there are almost 80 medical specialties). Our human existence is split into more than 80 different sections of medical science, and we have forgotten to notice the holistic view of us as a complete organism.

Nowadays, we identify ourselves primarily with the neocortex, thanks in no small part to the famous words of Descartes, "Cogito, ergo sum" ("I think, therefore I am"), which places great emphasis on our thinking and reasoning abilities, instead of our overall abilities as a living being.

23.

Makeup of our Three Brains and how they are connected

Let's start connecting the dots. We'll take a look at the research work that proves the connection and that explains how communication goes from the bottom to the top.

In his book In an Unspoken Voice, Peter Levine describes a 1948 paper by the Russian-born neuropathologist, Ivan Yakovlev, in which he hypothesized and introduced the concept that the central nervous system structures have evolved from bottom to top, as a result of our increasingly complex behaviors.[84]

Yakovlev argued that the most evolutionarily primitive brain structures we have in our head are the brainstem and hypothalamus. They regulate the internal states through autonomic control of the viscera and blood vessels. They form the matrix upon which the remainder of the brain, as well as behavior, is elaborated.

He also describes the limbic system. This system is related to emotions, our posture, movements and actions, as well as regulating our unconscious facial expressions and expressing the internal visceral states.

Finally, the neocortex. Yakovlev describes this as the outgrowth of the limbic system, which allows a conscious control of movement and actions, perception, symbolization, language and manipulation of the external environment, and all while managing our internal visceral states.

He emphasized that these Brains are overlapping and integrated parts that contribute to the organism's total behavior. The limbic system and neocortex are rooted in the primitive Gut Brainstem and are elaborations of its function.

It was Yakovlev's belief based on his research that the appearance of the more complex and highly ordered Head Brain (the cerebral cortex) is an evolutionary refinement, which was ultimately derived from emotional and visceral (gut) functions including ingestion, digestion, and elimination. Put simply, the Gut Brain is in charge.[85]

Lisa Barrett Feldman provides in her book Seven and a Half Lessons About the Brain a nice insight into how we are all originated.

She uses the amphioxus, a little worm with gill-like slits on either side of its body as a reference for how our Brains have developed. It lives on the seafloor stuck to the seafloor as a plant where it consumes any minuscule creatures that drift into its mouth. It does not have taste, smell or ears as they are not needed for this and eyes are just light detectors. It has a few wires that we could call a nervous system and a teeny clump of cells that if we use our imagination, functions as a control center or brain. As she writes, the amphioxus was a stomach on a stick.[86]

Daniel J Siegel, Clinical Professor of Psychiatry at the UCLA School of Medicine and Executive Director of the Mindsight Institute, writes in his book Mindsight, that "the heart has an extensive network of nerves that process complex information and relay data upward to the brain in the skull." Moreover, he shares that so too, do the intestines. "This data forms the foundation for visceral maps that help us have a 'gut feeling' or a 'heartfelt' sense. Such input from the body forms a vital source of intuition and powerfully influences our reasoning and the way we create meaning in our lives".[87]

In popular science you can often read about the Polyvagal Theory from Stephan Porges.[88] I have had many questions about how the Three Brains Theory connects with the Polyvagal Theory. In short, it does not as the Polyvagal Theory is scientifically debunked.[89] [90] [91] The nerve system works totally differently to how he proclaimed therefore there is no connection. Having said that, of course we have an Autonomic Nervous System (ANS).

To make it simple: the ANS is the highway for communication between our Three Brains and all the other cells in our body.

Autonomic nervous system

The Autonomic Nervous System is in contact with all the organs, muscles, and Brains, and is responsible for unconscious actions. It regulates the heart rate, digestion, respiratory rate, pupillary response, urination, sexual arousal and other fundamental bodily functions.

Our body has 3 complementary nervous systems to sustain life:

1. The sympathetic nervous system popularly called the Fight and flight nervous system is responsible for activating the body. The sympathetic nervous system connects the internal organs to the brain by spinal nerves. When stimulated, these nerves prepare the organism for stress by increasing the heart rate, increasing blood flow to the muscles, and decreasing blood flow to the skin.
2. The enteric nervous system which has a main functional control of visceral organs) and

3. The parasympathetic nervous system with is responsible for calming the body. The parasympathetic nervous system includes all the cranial nerves. In some literature the Parasympathetic Nervous system is divided into two systems, the Dorsal Vagal and Cranial Nerves. The dorsal vagus nerve is the oldest nerve in our body. It developed 500 million years ago and is present in all animals. It originally evolved in cold-blooded animals and had the primary function of immobilization, or rather shutting down, fainting, or hibernating. Later in evolution as we became more complex, warm blooded etc. Our Cranial Nerves became more evolved and especially the Cranial X or also called the ventral vagus nerve. The parasympathetic nervous system is responsible for the body's rest and digestion response when the body is relaxed, resting, or feeding. It basically undoes the work of sympathetic division after a stressful situation. The parasympathetic nervous system decreases respiration and heart rate and increases digestion. The Cranial X nerve, which emerges directly from the brain (including the brainstem) has a slightly different setup as the other cranial nerves as it dives deep in the body. One of cranial X nerve's role is relaying information between the brain and parts of the body. It functions primarily to and from the head and neck regions, including the senses of vision, taste, smell, and sound.

Through each of these three pathways, we react "in service of our survival and happiness." They control how we communicate with our partner, so understanding these pathways will help us better understand our partner.

Extremely important: Our nerves do not **decide** to activate/function by themselves.

4. A nerve is the axon or dendrites from a Neuron (brain cell) and can only be activated by the nucleus (the center) of the neuron or by a neuro-transmitter activating the synapsis. If one of those happens, an electric signal is transported through the Axon or Dendrites. If we massage or

put electricity on an axon or dendrites (the nerve) it also sends out a signal but it does not do that by itself.

Parasympathetic nervous system and the Cranial X, the magic one's

Now, we know that the dorsal and ventral branches of the vagus nerve originate from different locations in the brain and brainstem. They have separate pathways through the body and have different functions as well. What we know as the Ventral Vagal is actually the Cranial X.

There is no direct anatomical or functional connection between the two. They are separate and distinct entities.[92]

The two nerve systems travel in two different directions as well:

- upward, to connect with the nerves in the neck, throat, eyes, and ears.
- downward, through the lungs, heart, diaphragm, and stomach.

One of the objectives of the Gut brain is immobilization and that is communicated via the dorsal and Cranial X nerve. The primitive immobilization system originated approximately 500 million years ago, and we share this system with most vertebrates, as it stems from its origin in early fish species. It works in the following manner.

Immobilization means metabolic conservation and the process of shutdown. Its target of action is the internal organs, and conscious awareness. It turns the system into a hibernation state in extreme environments where food is not always available, and energy regulation is required. You can observe this with turtles or frogs in the winter. Their body temperature stays below five degrees Celsius. They have a minimal heartbeat and can stay like this for months. A beautiful instrument form the Gut Brain for survival.

Although it goes beyond the purpose of this book, from an evolutionary perspective there is a second reason for the Gut Brain and the dorsal nervous system. That second role is the protection of our conscious awareness (some call it 'soul' or 'spirit') from being hurt during extreme danger when we believe the only option is dying. It takes us out of our awareness and puts us into a protective state of collapse. When we feel frozen, numb, or 'not here', the Gut brain has taken control to protect us from suffering a painful death and is using the Dorsal and Cranial X to do so. Similarly, if you think about animals, for example when a lion hunts a deer, this nerve prevents the deer from feeling the pain of being killed, or when a fish is swallowed by a pelican, it protects the fish from the suffering of getting decomposed in the pelican's stomach acids.

We can observe an active dorsal nervous system and lesser activity of the all the cranial nerves also in people who are severely traumatized, and/or depressed.

Think back to when this immobilization may have happened to you. Maybe in the past, you had an aggressive discussion or a fight with someone, or went through a traumatic experience, and felt numb or did not know how to respond. It may have felt like your head brain was no longer operating. You may have almost fainted. This is our Gut Brain immobilization system in action.

Example: Disassociation response in action

I met with a patient once who had been through such a situation. She found out that her husband had been cheating on her for nearly six months, and he had decided to divorce her and live with the other woman.

She reported that the traumatic experience she had gone through made her feel like she had lost her mind for a while and had issues remembering those months. Also, she had sometimes felt as though she had left her physical body; she could see herself talking to her husband from a distance, and didn't feel as if she was really there.

She first thought she was crazy but learned that she was having disassociation reflexes.

If you remain in this dangerous state, when Gut Brain stays in a down state and the communication via the dorsal branch does not get turned off, the cranial nerves get activated again. It is usually because our Head Brain keeps receiving signals from the Gut Brain to analyze and therefore remember the trauma or event. It signals the Gut Brain to stay in that state of immobilization, even though the danger is not there anymore, leading to a chronic state of immobilization. This state is what we call 'depression'.

If you ever had a period of depression or sadness, you will know that a person in such a state feels depleted, without energy, and finds no joy in life. Such a person may face issues with seeing a happy future or may not feel any motivation to mobilize themselves again to do sports or even to live.

At that moment, your Gut Brain is active 24/7 and as it is signaling the Head Brain via the dorsal nerve, we can test it. When I see a depressed patient, I always test them for the activity of the dorsal nerve by examining the ventral vagus nerve. It is always a positive result. The ventral nerve is inactive, and the dorsal nerve is active in these cases. You can read more about this in Stanley Rosen's book, The Healing Power of the Vagus Nerve.[93]

Eighty million years ago, the ventral vagal pathway or cranial X nerve that is responsible for the muscles in our face became a more important part of our system. This nerve or pathway also transports the signals of safety and support, feelings of being safely engaged and socially connected from the Heart Brain. Understanding this is vital to understanding the logic behind the way humans communicate.

Research has made it clear that the Amygdala lights up 7 milliseconds after every heartbeat,[94] and as we know the Amygdala is the control center of emotions in our head.

This nerve is neuro-anatomically linked to the nerves that are in control of the facial expressions and vocalization. This system is in control of the muscles in the throat, face, middle ear, heart, and lungs, which all work together in communicating our emotions and feelings to others and ourselves.

What this means is that when this nerve is activated through the Heart Brain, we feel safe. It allows us to communicate much more from our heart, smile when others smile at us, nod our head when we agree with someone, and frown when friends tell us about their misfortunes. When the ventral nerve is active, we are open to establishing a connection with another person.

The other side of the coin is the sympathetic nervous system. This came to the world in the period of reptilians, about 300 million years ago. Like everything in us, it is based on survival but with the addition of the famous 'fight-or-flight' action. It responds to what we personally perceive as cues of danger and triggers the release of adrenaline, which fuels the fight-or-flight response.

It works on the primary muscles to activate them. It is our system of action for mobilization. A major difference in our nervous system is that the sympathetic nervous system is not directly connected with the brainstem. The sympathetic nerves are located in the middle of the back between our neck and our waist. From there, they extend out to communicate with the related organs, such as eyes, heart, lungs, stomach, bladder, and genitals.

It is understandable that the sympathetic nerves may communicate with genitals, as that explains why people can commit crimes like rape. Rape is not an act of love, but an act of anger or fearful lust.

For an insight into how you and your partner are affected when you perceive danger in communication, let's take a look at the following facts.

The so-called sympathetic adrenal medullary system (SAM) is the quick responder. Within 100 milliseconds, it sends out communication back and forth for a short-term, rapid response, almost a shock and awe, and is followed by a return to regulation. We can observe this in animals when they perceive danger: their pupils dilate, and their body is ready to run. When they realize it was just a false alarm, they directly return to the state of relaxation. You might have experienced a situation with your partner where they may have said something to you, and you might have felt like they were making fun of you or was saying something serious. Your immediate response to that would be something like, "What did you say to me?" However, you realized that your partner was joking in a matter of seconds.

When you do not misunderstand what your partner said, the hypothalamic–pituitary–adrenal (HPA) axis takes over when this quick, adrenaline-fueled surge of energy does not resolve the distress. The HPA axis releases cortisol, commonly called the 'stress hormone'. This release takes longer and is slower to take effect, requiring minutes rather than seconds, because the hormones are released in the bloodstream and therefore, this state of arousal can last for hours.

How can you tell when the so-called SAM or HPA axis are in action? Some of the things we can observe in others or ourselves are pupil dilation, sweating, progressively increasing reactions like breathing and heart rates, fighting or fleeing (physically or verbally).[95]

EXAMPLE: LONG-TERM IMMOBILIZATION DUE TO A TRAUMATIC PAST EVENT

My client had been to a party at a friend's house. She initially enjoyed her time with people — laughing, feeling content and connected. This means that she felt safe and her social connecting nerve was active, so her Heart Brain was allowed to be in charge.

Later in the evening, some people got drunk, and one of them became abusive towards her, so she started to feel threatened. She connected with others at the party to find help, support, and comfort from the people around her. She instinctively turned to the first level of protection, which is social engagement. This means her Gut Brain became alert and her first reaction was to flee the predator and seek protection.

Most of the time the story ends here; the drunk people are displaced from the party or calmed down, and everything goes back to normal. She stayed over at the party, and while it was still busy, she went to bed as she agreed with her friend that she would stay over in a guest room. Somebody entered her room, silenced her by putting a hand on her mouth, and threatened to hurt her if she said something.

Therefore, no one could come to her aid, she was in immediate danger. Her Gut Brain and sympathetic nervous system took action and was signaling a more primitive way to survive: fight or flight. She did her best to fight off the attacker, by trying to push him off her. Unfortunately, her effort didn't work; she tried to escape, but that did not work either. She could not get away as she was held down and trapped. She said, "It was like I stepped outside myself — like I preserved myself by shutting down and spending as little energy as possible. She entered a state of helplessness and hopelessness when she finally collapsed.

The result was that after being sexually abused, nothing even worse happened to her. The predator only did what he came to do, and because she looked lifeless, he disappeared. Also because of the shutdown, she did not have any Head Brain recollection about what actually happened after she immobilized herself. That does not mean she did not experience trauma after that. However, she got hurt as little as possible considering the horrendous situation.

Because of the imprint this incident left on her Gut Brain and Heart Brain, she experienced relationship issues. For the first few years after this awful event, the Gut Brain kept the Heart Brain in a shutdown state, and she was unable to engage in an emotionally connecting relationship. It also meant that she always wanted to be in control of a relationship, so she participated in one-night stands or over-week-end relationships, to prove to herself that she was the boss. And, last but not least, she had issues with being held, cuddled and other romantic gestures that made her feel like she was trapped.

I'm happy to share that she realized the cause of how she was feeling, did a lot of self-work, visited other psychologists besides me, and through all of her hard work, she was able to rediscover her 'normal' self once again. She is now able to live again with trust, to connect from the Heart Brain and to have a healthy, romantic relationship.

When you think of yourself, what kind of dislikes do you still have from previous experiences that logically should not be there anymore, but still pop up unexpectedly?

As mentioned earlier, this shutdown behavior or constant fight-or-flight behavior can be observed in people who are severely depressed or highly anxious. Depressed people live in a frozen or collapsed state; they don't have the energy to do anything, not even to get out of bed. Since the shut-down system is active, the Heart Brain's connecting capacity is turned off, both towards ourselves and others. The Head Brain cannot analyze what happened or find a solution and is therefore mostly in overdrive remuner-ating or overanalyzing. And, last but not least, the Gut Brain turned off the connection with the self-awareness in the Head Brain. In this state it is almost impossible for the person to feel something or find a solution.

In 2004, Dr Ruth Lanius did some research with people who had suffered serious childhood abuse. She found that there was almost no activation of any of the self-sensing areas of the Head Brain.[96]

Such people are essentially trapped in their bodies.

Anxious people are always on the move, because the fight or flight response is sending out orders for all those movements and the blood flow to the main muscles pushes them to perform a related action.

Besides having this nervous system that communicates bottom-up and top-down, how does the heart or the gut know what is happening?

It is quite interesting to see how our gut communicates. In 2010, neuro-scientist Diego Bohórquez of Duke University in Durham, North Carolina, made a startling discovery.[97] Enteroendocrine cells, that stud the lining of our gut, produce hormones that spur digestion and suppress hunger, and have feet-like protrusions resembling the synapses that neurons use to communicate with each other. Bohórquez knew that the enteroendocrine cells could send hormonal messages to the central nervous system. He and his colleagues injected a fluorescent rabies virus, which is transmit-ted through neuronal synapses, into the colons of mice and waited for these cells and their partners to light up. Those partners turned out to be to vagal neurons.

In a petri dish, enteroendocrine cells reached out to vagal neurons and formed synaptic connections with each other. The cells even gushed out a glutamate, which is a neurotransmitter involved in smelling and tasting. The vagal neurons picked up glutamate within 100 milliseconds. That is faster than the blink of an eye.

These gut sensory cells date back to one of the first multicellular organisms; a flat creature called Trichoplax adhaerens, which emerged roughly 600 million years ago.

Researchers used lasers to stimulate the sensory neurons that innervate the gut in mice, which produced rewarding sensations, causing the rodents to work hard to repeat the reward. The researchers also found that laser stimulation also increased levels of a mood-boosting neurotransmitter called dopamine in the rodents' Brains. So light is used as communication in the gut.[98] [99]

24.

Other methods of communication, light, & energy

We know that the Gut Brain and the Heart Brain are in constant and extensive communication with the Head Brain. Ninety percent of the communication goes bottom-up, and that information is first collected in the brainstem. Then it is redirected to the Cerebellum and Brain Stem brain and limbic brain before it is sent to the 'right' parts in the human brain. Therefore, the Head Brain is the last one to know.[100]

How do the Gut Brain and the Heart Brain sense? How do they collect their data from the outside world or even from the inside world? How does neuroception work?

Just think about a flock of birds flying. Thousands of birds fly together as if they are one living organism. How about shoals of fish in the sea that move like one organism?

How do these birds or fish communicate? They cannot move as one without having effective communication with each other, but they don't communicate in the ways we know. It is like they know without knowing; they communicate without communicating.

To understand how your Gut Brain or Heart Brain know without knowing is based on the same principle.

Science has not yet found a definitive answer to exactly how this works, but progress is being made, via the strange world of energy fields and even quantum physics.

It has been found that we have 'radar' for this in our heart and gut.

Scientific proof for this is published in the meta research of predicting the unpredictable, critical analysis, and practical implications of predictive anticipatory activity.[101]

These studies also prove that we humans can predict what is going to happen one to ten seconds before it really happens.

How is that possible if we can only use our known senses like smell, eyesight or hearing? It occurs because we have receptors, like a radar or an antenna, that can detect energy from the outside and inside world.

In his book Kinesiology and Applied Kinesiology, Robert Frost describes the five methods of communication in our body with which we can inter-connect internally and externally:[102]

1. Chemical signals: hormones
2. Electric impulses through the nervous system
3. Electrochemical synapses (between functional organs, cells helping them act together)
4. Electromagnetic vibrations (sent out by the heart, can be measured nine meters outside the person)
5. Light, biophoton emissions (sent out by every cell)

Examples of Electromagnetic vibrations can be found in the book, Clinical Applications of Bioelectromagnetic Medicine, in which Rollin McCarty, PhD, wrote a chapter about electromagnetic fields generated by the heart.[103]

He describes the electromagnetic fields that are generated by the heart and permeate every cell in our body, which may act as a synchronizing signal for the body in a manner that is analogous to information carried by radio waves. He demonstrates that this energy is not only transmitted internally to the brain, but it is also detectable by others within its range of communication. The heart generates the largest electromagnetic field in the body.

He explains that when this electrical field is measured in an electrocardiogram (ECG), it is about 60 times greater in amplitude than our brainwaves recorded in an electroencephalogram (EEG). The magnetic component of our heart's field, which is around 5,000 times stronger than that produced by the brain, is not impeded by tissues and can be measured several feet away from the body with Superconducting Quantum Interference Device (SQUID)-based magnetometers. They have also found that the clear rhythmic patterns in beat-to-beat heart rate variability are distinctly altered when different emotions are experienced. These changes in electromagnetic, sound, and blood pressure waves produced by cardiac rhythmic activity are 'felt' by every cell in the body, further supporting the heart's role as a global internal synchronizing signal.

In the book "The science of the heart" by Heartmath, it stated that research demonstrated that the heart has ways of communicating with the brain and body: Neurological communication (nervous system) Biochemical communication (hormones) Biophysical communication (pulse wave) Energetic communication (electromagnetic fields)[104] and as shared before, the Amygdala lights up 7 milliseconds after every heartbeat,[105] as if the heart is sharing it is alright or it is not okay.

In the same book is it shared that evidence now supports the perspective that a subtle yet influential electromagnetic or "energetic" communication system operates just below our conscious level of awareness.

Dr Rollin McCraty from Heartmath shares research in the Heart Series that was broadcasted on channel 4[106] that the heart responds before the mind knows. This section of the broadcast starts around minute 36 into the video.

In her books The Intention Experiment[107] and The Bond, Lynne McTaggart shares research and examples of the power of connection, and how we can communicate without the obvious communication methods. She shares scientific experiments in which people were somehow able to receive the thoughts and emotions of another person, even when they were in different rooms separated by concrete walls.

The 'issue' with all of this is that in medical science when they cannot find real evidence of how it works, how the body cells emit or receive the electromagnetic vibrations or the biophoton energy, they find it hard to believe that we can receive and communicate in this way. If you would like to know how it is possible that we can communicate in that way, quantum biology or quantum mechanics provides some insight.

The most insightful and convincing example is the entanglement theory. This theory is based on the premise that photons (light/energy) which start off connected, are sent away in exactly opposite directions, (they move with the speed of light whilst staying connected).[108] They act as if they are still one when something happens with one of the photons. When the rotation is changing in one photon, precisely the same happens to the other photon.

According to Einstein, the speed of light is the fastest speed in this universe. And still, when those two photons move at the speed of light in opposite directions, they are still able to "communicate" with each other. In research this behavior of photons is already observed. In a research facility in the USA, they send information from one atom to another without them being physically connected. They entangle the atoms by synchronizing the photons in the atom, and then the information from one atom is sent to the other, without any perceived communication or connection between the two atoms.[109] [110]

Photons are extremely small particles that are perceived as light or a little bundle of energy; no receptors, no mouth, no nose to smell, nothing of that sort, and they can still "communicate" with each other.

So, although we cannot explain exactly how this works, our body is reacting to energy from the outside world and communicates to itself in the same way. Every cell sends out photons, and other cells receive this information and take action.

In the YouTube series, The Secrets of Quantum Physics: Let There Be Life, Professor Jim Al-Khalili shows how plants used quantum physics in pursuing energy when light comes into their chlorophyll cells.[111]

In The Bond, Lynne McTaggart describes the research of the German physicist, Fritz Albert Popp, and his work with biophoton emission.[112] And this is mind-blowing, I can tell you.

Fritz Albert Popp was investigating a cure for cancer in the 1970s, and found that all living organisms, from single-celled plants to human beings, emit a tiny current of photons, or light. He introduced this phenomenon as 'biophoton emissions'.

Popp theorized that living organisms could make use of this faint light as a way of communication, between the cells of the organism, and also with the outside world.

After 30 years of research by Popp, and more than 40 other scientists around the globe, there is complete belief that this faint radiation of energy is the primary conductor of all cellular processes in the body. Therefore, our DNA or biochemistry is not entirely responsible for cellular processes.[113]

"Cohen and Popp have also discovered that biophoton emissions happen within our DNA, setting off certain frequencies within the molecules of individual cells"

In one of their experiments, they discovered something peculiar. When ointment was applied to one part of the body, the light emissions from that part of the body changed massively and other parts of the body started to send out the same light.

From that moment on, Popp knew for sure that he had discovered a communication channel within living organisms, namely, using light as a means of instantaneous communication.

In further research, Popp proved that these light emissions act as a communication system between living things. In several experiments from plants to human beings, he discovered that an individual living thing absorbs the light emitted from the other and sends back wave-interference patterns, as though they are having a conversation. Once the light waves of one organism are absorbed by another organism, the first organism's light begins trading information in synchrony.[114] [115]

This is the way our gut bacteria communicate with our Heart Brain or Head Brain, or other parts of our body. These 'conversations' also occur between different species, although the loudest and the best are reserved for members of the same species.

In conclusion regarding communication, our Heart Brain and our Gut Brain communicate with our Head Brain, using hormones and the nervous system. The heart also uses electromagnetic vibrations to communicate, and if that is not enough, the Heart and Gut Brains are well-developed enough to communicate with biophoton emissions.

I think it is fair to say that what Ivan Yakovlev hypothesized in 1948, namely that the appearance of the more complex and highly ordered Head Brain as an evolutionary refinement, is entirely accurate. Ultimately, the Head Brain is derived from the emotional Heart Brain and survival Gut Brain. And if it were the other way round, the Head Brain would be in charge of the other two Brains, and other parts of the body.

25.

Recap, last words and a request

I hope you enjoyed reading this book as much as I did writing it.

Also, I hope and sincerely wish that you learned what you wanted to learn and that it will improve your relationships with your partner, your family, your friends, and colleagues.

My request to you is to please spread the word, share it on social media, maybe pass on your favorite quotes, lessons learned or examples from this book.

This will not only make your life better, but also the lives of the people around you.

I have an expansive dream; it will make this world a better place to live. With less bullying, fighting, and hurting, and one where we behave with the belief that men and women are from the same planet and that only their Three Brains may act differently. I believe that this will indeed achieve a much more sharing, caring and loving world for us all to live in.

If you would like to share your stories or comments, I would love to hear or read them.

Of course, you can follow me on social media for the latest updates and downloads:

Facebook: https://www.facebook.com/ChristoffelSneijders/
LinkedIn: https://www.linkedin.com/in/christoffel
YouTube: youtube.com/@01christoffel
Twitter: http://www.twitter.com/chrissneijders
Instagram: https://www.instagram.com/christoffelsneijders/

If you like to master truly how you can coach and assist others using the Three Brains. How about joining the: Three Brains coach Certification Training, you can find them on
https://www.3brainsacademy.com/

ACKNOWLEDGEMENTS

When I first had the idea of writing this book, I procrastinated, partly due to self-doubt. What could I add to the thousands of self-help books that have already been written? Books written by great people about relationships, communication and coaching.

I did know that something was missing in all of them but how could I verbalize that? Being dyslexic, all my life I have heard that I am bad at language and writing skills. Ask me to write down a word like 'thorough' or say a word of more than three syllables and you will be entertained. So, writing a book would be a huge challenge to say the least.

I know now that these thoughts were actually coming from one part of my brain; it was my Gut Brain which was protecting my Heart Brain from rejection and judgment.

Having said that, I am grateful to that little boy in the hospital without whom I would never have been able to write this book. Along with the little boy, I am grateful to one of my clients who sent me the following letter as a gesture of thanks for what I did for her. She wrote,

"When I walked into Christoffel's office, I was in a very bad place. I was suffering from depression that was physically weighing me down. I had to take the week off from work because I couldn't cope. I was looking for something, anything, to help me stop drinking because that was making everything worse. I was drinking two

bottles of wine a day. Although there have been periods where I was doing slightly better, I'd pretty much been drinking that much every day for 10 years. I'm on antidepressants and had been seeing a psychologist for five years, but none of that was working. I was desperate for help and I started more unhappy and unhealthy relationships than I could count.

Christoffel asked me to tell him what my issues were. Now, because I had been talking to a psychologist, I was able to tell him the following points:

As a child, I had felt unloved by my mother. I had learned that it was important to be invisible, to make sure I focused on, and delivered, what other people needed, so as to be safe.

I had intrusive visions of a sexual assault by my brother and a friend of his when I was a child. I didn't know if they were real or not, but they wouldn't go away, and I kept pushing them down, ignoring them.

Twenty-two years ago, I became pregnant (when I had believed, and grieved over, the fact that I couldn't get pregnant) but I was not in a relationship and in a panic, I arranged an abortion. I was sobbing as I was taken into theater but nobody stopped to ask if I wanted to go ahead. I hated myself for that decision and continued to do so.

I felt I didn't deserve happiness, that I was unworthy. I hated myself.

Unbelievably for me, Christoffel was able to help me bring the little girl who felt unloved up out of my Gut and into my Heart. I could see her and feel her energy moving. I promised her I would love her and take care of her. I forgave myself.

And I was able to bring myself up from my hidden places, the trauma of the images of sexual abuse, my feelings of being complicit in what had happened to that little girl, my anger and grief over it. I was able to accept that those things, and my decision to abort my child, were a part of what made me who I am, that all those feelings, my decisions, were understandable, and that I should truly forgive myself.

At the end of the session, I was able to say, and for the first time ever, I believe, that I love myself and I forgive myself. The weight of depression miraculously lifted off of me. I came in, unable to smile, hunched in on myself, unable to cope with life, and I left grinning and happy.

I felt, literally, a million times better!

I can't thank Christoffel enough. And I hope other people can have the opportunity to have their lives turned around like me because of him."

After receiving this letter, I decided to call her and share my idea of writing a book based on my knowledge about the Three Brains. She made sure to convince me enough to bring the idea into practice.

My heart goes out to this client, just as it goes out to my students who 'pushed' me to share my knowledge, the bullies at school, previous relationships, the good and bad times and the breakups, which taught me how we as human beings, of all genders, think, communicate, love, hate, and feel everything else. I am grateful to have experienced that and have (had) them in my life. Without them I would not be the person I am now.

Special thanks go out to my partner Maria Teresa Alonso Jaen, Lisa Newlin, Diana Vere who motivated me to make this second edition and Ann McGregor who undertook the challenging task to make it proper English. Of course, to all the students of the Three Brains Coaching Certification Training who gave me trust and played with the concepts shared in this book.

Last but not least, all the people I have met in my life who shared their stories whilst having a coffee or on a plane.

My dream and wish are that this book helps you to change, to develop and to create a better version of yourself, and have a better relationship with your partner, parents, friends, colleagues, and kids.

ABOUT CHRISTOFFEL

I am extremely passionate to bring out the best in you.

Always curious about how our mind/body/spirit connection works and how that relates to our (personal) leadership, and our relationships with others.

With this vision in mind, I introduced the Three Brains–Head, Heart and Gut–Theory in 2016 after many years of research into how to best to assist clients who remained stuck in limiting beliefs and trauma like experiences.

I am teaching these concepts in the ICF CCEU approved Three Brains Coaching Certification Training, at the IE business School, and I am the author of the book you have just read 😃

My passion, authenticity, empathy, and versatile knowledge in Hypnosis, NLP, Coaching, psychotherapy burnout, PTSD, anxiety, trauma and grief are vital to helping my global clients create a life and outcomes they long for.

Working with so many people in a direct way has given me amazing insight into the ways in which we are similar, how we differ in our (personal) leadership, happiness and suffering, and how we can attain healthy success by creating an environment of integrated Head, Heart and Gut Brain connection.

SOURCES AND NOTES

1 https://www.researchgate.net/publication/261605461_Predicting_
theunpredictable_Critical_analysis_and_practical_implications_of_
predictive_anticipatory_activity

2 https://openoregon.pressbooks.pub/bodyphysics/chapter/
human-metabolism/

3 World Economic Forum, Briony Harris, These are the happiest countries
in the world, 2018, Website: https://www.weforum.org/agenda/2018/03/
these-are-the-happiest-countries-in-the-world/

4 World Happiness Report, 2018, Website: http://worldhappiness.
report/ed/2018/

5 Martin Seligman, (2010), Flourish,: Positive Psychology and Positive
Interventions, Website: https://tannerlectures.utah.edu/_documents/a-to-z/s/
Seligman_10.pdf

6 Gallup, Melanie Standish and Dan Witters, Country Well-Being Varies
Greatly Worldwide, (2014), Website: https://news.gallup.com/poll/175694/
country-varies-greatly-worldwide.aspx

7 https://filmsite.org/boxofffice.html 2019

8 Mental Health Information, Prevalence of Any Anxiety Disorder Among
Adults, (2017), Website: https://www.nimh.nih.gov/health/statistics/
any-anxiety-disorder.shtml

9 Machiavelli, N. (1532)–The Prince, as cited at: https://en.wikipedia.org/wiki/
The_Prince

10 Trillion Dollar Coach: The Leadership Playbook of Silicon Valley's Bill Campbell Hardcover – April 16, 2019 by Eric Schmidt (Author), Jonathan Rosenberg (Author), Alan Eagle (Author)

11 https://ncse.com/library-resource/definitions-fact-theory-law-scientific-work

12 Shendruk, A. (2017). Analyzing the Gender Representation of 34,476 Comic Book Characters. The Pudding. Retrieved from: https://pudding.cool/2017/07/comics/

13 Clearly Cultural, Masculinity, Website: http://clearlycultural.com/geert-hofstede-cultural-dimensions/masculinity/

14 NRC, Andreas Kouwenhoven, Dutch Woman in the Top of Interpol, (2018), Website: https://www.nrc.nl/nieuws/2018/11/21/nederlandse-vrouw-in-de-top-van-interpol-a2756092

15 Source http://healthland.time.com/2011/08/30/the-math-gender-gap-nurture-can-trump-nature/ written by Maia Szalavitz is a neuroscience journalist for TIME.com)

16 [1]Divorce Statistics: Over 115 Studies, Facts and Rates For 2018, (2017) Retrieved From:

   https://www.wf-lawyers.com/divorce-statistics-and-facts/

17 NSVRC: National Sexual Violence Resource Center, Statistics and Sexual Violence (2015), USA. Website: https://www.nsvrc.org/sites/default/files/publications_nsvrc_factsheet_media-packet_statistics-about-sexual-violence_0.pdf

18 Singh, M. M., Parsekar, S. S., & Nair, S. N. (2014). An epidemiological overview of child sexual abuse. Journal of family medicine and primary care, 3(4), 430. Website: https://www.ncbi.nlm.nih.gov/pmc/articles/PMC4311357/

19   The Body Keeps the Score: Brain, Mind, and Body in the Healing of Trauma Van Der Kolk, Bessel, https://besselvanderkolk.net/the-body-keeps-the-score.html

20   2015. https://nces.ed.gov/fastfacts/display.asp?id=719 https://nces.ed.gov/pubs2017/2017015.pdf

21   Peter A. Levine, (2010), In An Unspoken Voice, North Atlantic Books, ISBN: 9781556439438

22   https://en.wikipedia.org/wiki/Hebbian_theory, **Neurons that fire together, wire together.** Neuropsychologist **Donald Hebb** first used this phrase in 1949 to describe how pathways in the brain are formed and reinforced through repetition.

23   https://wis-wander.weizmann.ac.il/employeeold/neuroscience?page=8

24   Schaefer, J. D., Caspi, A., Belsky, D. W., Harrington, H., Houts, R., Horwood, L. J., ... & Moffitt, T. E. (2017). Enduring mental health: Prevalence and prediction. Journal of abnormal psychology, 126(2), 212. Retrieved from: https://www.ncbi.nlm.nih.gov/pmc/articles/PMC5304549/

25   NAMI: National Alliance on Mental Illness. (2018). Website: https://www.nami.org/#

26   WHO: World Health Organization. (2001). Mental disorders affect one in four people: Treatment available but not being used. World Health Report 2001. Retrieved from: https://www.who.int/whr/2001/media_centre/press_release/en/

27   Van der Kolk, B. A. (1994). The body keeps the score: Memory and the evolving psychobiology of posttraumatic stress. Harvard review of psychiatry, 1(5), 253-265. Website: https://www.tandfonline.com/doi/abs/10.3109/10673229409017088

28   NSVRC: National Sexual Violence Resource Center, Statistics and Sexual Violence (2015), USA. Website: https://www.nsvrc.org/sites/default/files/

publications_nsvrc_factsheet_media-packet_statistics-about-sexual-violence_0.pdf

29 https://youtu.be/H4BNbHBcnDI Finding Nemo: seagulls try to catch nemo

30 https://psychclassics.yorku.ca/Maslow/motivation.htm

31 Source https://youtu.be/VQr8xDk_UaY Puffer fish on the BBC

32 Source https://youtu.be/VQr8xDk_UaY Puffer fish on the BBC

33 2002 by Malcolm Gladwell The Tipping Point. ISBN: 978-0-7595-7473-1

34 https://youtu.be/drTiv5r57nI Hachi, A Dog's Tale trailer.

35 https://youtu.be/PCtkq-IRRNE video about Edison's mother

36 Quigley, B. M., & Tedeschi, J. T. (1996). Mediating effects of blame attributions on feelings of anger. Personality and Social Psychology Bulletin, 22(12), 1280-1288. Website:

37 Peter A. Levine, (2010), In An Unspoken Voice, North Atlantic Books, ISBN: 9781556439438

38 URL to the video: https://www.youtube.com/watch?v=-4EDhdAHrOg&feature=youtu.be

39 URL to the video: https://www.youtube.com/watch?v=-4EDhdAHrOg&feature=youtu.be

40 Rosenberg, Marshall B. Nonviolent Communication: A Language of Life, 3rd Edition: Life-Changing Tools for Healthy Relationships (Nonviolent Communication Guides).

41 Dotlich, D. L., Cairo, P. C., & Rhinesmith, S. H. (2010). Head, Heart and Guts: How the world's best companies develop complete leaders. John Wiley & Sons.

42 (source https://www.nimh.nih.gov/health/statistics/any-anxiety-disorder.shtml and

https://www.ncbi.nlm.nih.gov/pmc/articles/PMC4610617/

43   https://www.gottman.com/blog/the-four-horsemen-contempt/

44   Rosenberg, Marshall B. Nonviolent Communication: A Language of Life, 3rd Edition: Life-Changing Tools for Healthy Relationships (Nonviolent Communication Guides). PuddleDancer Press.

45   The 7 Habits of Highly Effective People, 1989, Stephen Covey ISBN 0-7432-6951-9

46   https://www.urmc.rochester.edu/encyclopedia/content. aspx?ContentTypeID=1&ContentID=3051

47   https://www.reuters.com/article/us-afghanistan-maternity-fb/factbox-why-are-maternal-deaths-so-high-in-afghanistan-idUSTRE7BB0FJ20111212

48   source https://embryology.med.unsw.edu.au/embryology/index.php/ Neural_-_Cranial_Nerve_Development

49   https://embryology.med.unsw.edu.au/embryology/index.php/ Gastrointestinal_Tract_-_Intestine_Development

50   Discovering the Brain. ContentsHardcopy Version at National Academies Press

51   Neuroscience for children, Eric H. Chudler, University of Washington, Brain Development, (2015), Website: https://faculty.washington.edu/ chudler/dev.html.

52   http://www.bbbgeorgia.org/brainConnections.php

53   Mental Floss, Jordan Rosenfeld, 10 Amazing Facts About the Infant Brain, (2015), Website: http://mentalfloss.com/ article/70105/10-amazing-facts-about-infant-Brain

54   "The Brain & the Mind." Psychology Volume 1. 2002: 117.

55   https://www.healyourlife.com/are-you-programmed-at-birth, Are You Programmed at Birth? Bruce H. Lipton Ph.D.

56 Gamma Mindset, An example of just how EASY it is to IMPRINT a BELIEF into a young child's mind! (2016), Website: https://www.gammamindset. com/example-just-easy-imprint-belief-young-childs-mind/

57 https://www.pediatrics.emory.edu/divisions/neurology/education/ pedeeg.html

58 The Body Keeps the Score: Brain, Mind, and Body in the Healing of Trauma Van Der Kolk, Bessel, https://besselvanderkolk.net/the-body-keeps-the-score.html

59 Van der Kolk, B. A. (1994). The body keeps the score: Memory and the evolving psychobiology of posttraumatic stress. Harvard review of psychiatry, 1(5), 253-265. Website: https://www.tandfonline.com/doi/abs/10.3109/10673229409017088

60 Van der Kolk, B. A. (1994). The body keeps the score: Memory and the evolving psychobiology of posttraumatic stress. Harvard review of psychiatry, 1(5), 253-265. Website: https://www.tandfonline.com/doi/abs/10.3109/10673229409017088

61 Van der Kolk, B. A. (1994). The body keeps the score: Memory and the evolving psychobiology of posttraumatic stress. Harvard review of psychiatry, 1(5), 253-265. Website: https://www.tandfonline.com/doi/abs/10.3109/10673229409017088

62 12. P. M. Crittenden, "IV Peering into the Black Box: An Exploratory Treatise on the Development of Self in Young Children," Disorders and Dysfunctions of the Self 5 (1994): 79; P. M. Crittenden, and A. Landini, Assessing Adult Attachment: A Dynamic-Maturational Approach to Discourse Analysis

63 13. Patricia M. Crittenden, "Children's Strategies for Coping with Adverse Home Environments: An Interpretation Using Attachment Theory,"

64 https://en.wikipedia.org/wiki/Waldorf_education

65 Neurocardiology Hardcover – January 15, 1994 by J. Andrew Armour (Editor), Jeffrey L. Ardell https://fohs.bgu.ac.il/develop/DB2/Heart%20 memory/Armour,%202007.pdf

(Editor). https://www.researchgate.net/ publication/307410420_The_intellectual_heart.)

66 https://www.omicsonline.org/open-access/cardiovascular-action-of-oxytocin-2161-0479.1000e124.php?aid=33253

67 https://www.heartmath.org/research/science-of-the-heart/ heart-brain-communication/

68 The transplanted heart;: The incredible story of the epic heart transplant operations by Professor Christiaan Barnard and his team Hardcover – 1968

69 https://www.heartmath.org/research/science-of-the-heart/ heart-brain-communication/

70 McCraty, R., Atkinson, M., Tomasino, D. and Bradley, R. T., The coherent heart: Heart-brain interactions, psychophysiological coherence, and the emergence of system-wide order. Integral Review, 2009. 5(2): p. 10-115

71 McCraty, R., M. Atkinson, and R.T. Bradley, Electrophysiological evidence of intuition: Part 2. A system-wide process? J Altern Complement Med, 2004. 10(2): p. 325-326

72 McCraty, R., The energetic heart: Bioelectromagnetic communication within and between people, in Bioelectromagnetic Medicine, P.J. Rosch and M.S. Markov, Editors. 2004, Marcel Dekker: New York. p. 541-562.

73 Claude Bernard Principes de médecine expérimentale 1865 Neurosci Biobehav Rev. 2009 Feb;33(2):81-8. doi: 10.1016/j.neubiorev.2008.08.004. Epub 2008 Aug 13. Claude Bernard and the heart-brain connection: further elaboration of a model of neurovisceral integration. Thayer JF1, Lane RD. The Ohio State University, Department of Psychology, 1835 Neil Avenue, Columbus, OH 43210, USA. Thayer.39@osu.edu)

74 (Darwin C. The Expression of Emotions in Man and Animals. D Appleton; New York, NY: 1872)

75 The Second Brain: A Groundbreaking New Understanding of Nervous Disorders of the Stomach and Intestine by Michael Gershon (Author) ISBN-13: 978-0060930721 ISBN-10: 0060930721

76 https://www.caltech.edu/about/news/microbes-help-produce-serotonin-gut-46495

77 https://pubmed.ncbi.nlm.nih.gov/33803407/

78 https://www.ncbi.nlm.nih.gov/pubmed/29360467

79 https://www.sciencenews.org/article/parkinsons-disease-gut-microbes-brain-link

80 In an Unspoken Voice: How the Body Releases Trauma and Restores Goodness Paperback – September 28, 2010 by Peter A. Levine (Author), Gabor Mate (Foreword)

81 Barrett, Lisa Feldman. Seven and a Half Lessons About the Brain (p. 1). Pan Macmillan UK. Kindle Edition.

82 Soosalu, Grant. mBraining–Using your multiple Brains to do cool stuff. TimeBinding Publications.

83 https://www.youtube.com/watch?v=ktkjUjcZid0&t=253s MIND FIELD The Cognitive Tradeoff Hypothesis Tetsuro Matsuzawa

84 Source Peter Levine an unspoken voice, North Atlantic books 2010

85 Source Peter Levine an unspoken voice, North Atlantic books 2010

86 Barrett, Lisa Feldman. Seven and a Half Lessons About the Brain (p. 6). Pan Macmillan UK. Kindle Edition.

87 Source Siegel, Daniel J. Mindsight: change your brain and your life. 9781921753954

88 Porges, Stephen W. The Polyvagal Theory: Neurophysiological Foundations of Emotions, Attachment, Communication, and Self-regulation (Norton Series on Interpersonal Neurobiology). W. W. Norton & Company. ISBN 978-0-393-70700-7

89 https://www.researchgate.net/post/After-20-years-of-polyvagal-hypotheses-is-there-any-direct-evidence-for-the-first-3-premises-that-form-the-foundation-of-the-polyvagal-conjectures

90 https://www.osteopathie-liem.de/blog/critique-of-the-polyvagal-theory/

91 https://teachmeanatomy.info/head/cranial-nerves/vagus-nerve-cn-x/

92 Rosenberg, Stanley. Accessing the Healing Power of the Vagus Nerve: Self-Help Exercises for Anxiety, Depression, Trauma, and Autism (p. iv). North Atlantic Books. ISBN 978-1-62317-024-0

93 Rosenberg, Stanley. Accessing the Healing Power of the Vagus Nerve: Self-Help Exercises for Anxiety, Depression, Trauma, and Autism (p. iv). North Atlantic Books. ISBN 978-1-62317-024-0

94 Hopkins, D. and H. Ellenberger, Cardiorespiratory neurons in the mudulla oblongata: Input and output relationhsips , in Neurocardiology , J.A. Armour and J.L. Ardell, Editors. 1994, Oxford University Press: New York. p. 219-244. Science of the Heart. Science of the Heart (Kindle Location 3108-3109).

95 Porges, Stephen W. The Polyvagal Theory: Neurophysiological Foundations of Emotions, Attachment, Communication, and Self-regulation. W. W. Norton & Company. 2011

96 Kolk, Bessel van der. The Body Keeps the Score: Mind, Brain and Body in the Transformation of Trauma . paragraph "how do we know we are alive"

97 Website: https://www.sciencedaily.com/releases/2018/09/180920161011.htm

98 Website: http://science.sciencemag.org/content/361/6408/eaat5236

99 Website: https://www.sciencemag.org/news/2018/09/ your-gut-directly-connected-your-brain-newly-discovered-neuron-circuit

100 11. J. LeDoux, "Rethinking the Emotional Brain," Neuron 73, no. 4 (2012): 653–76. See also J. S. Feinstein, et al., "The Human Amygdala and the Induction and Experience of Fear," Current Biology 21, no. 1 (2011): 34–38. 12. The medial

101 https://www.researchgate.net/publication/261605461_Predicting_ theunpredictable_Critical_analysis_and_practical_implications_of_ predictive_anticipatory_activity

102 Frost Ph.D., Robert. Applied Kinesiology, Revised Edition. North Atlantic Books. eISBN: 978-1-58394-629-9

103 Clinical Applications of Bioelectromagnetic Medicine **Author:** McCraty R https://www.qigonginstitute.org/abstract/3032/ clinical-applications-of-bioelectromagnetic-medicine

104 Science of the Heart. Science of the Heart (Kindle Locations 90-92)

105 Hopkins, D. and H. Ellenberger, Cardiorespiratory neurons in the mudulla oblongata: Input and output relationhsips , in Neurocardiology , J.A. Armour and J.L. Ardell, Editors. 1994, Oxford University Press: New York. p. 219-244. Science of the Heart. Science of the Heart (Kindle Location 3108-3109).

106 https://youtu.be/ml1Ml49Y19Q

107 McTaggart, Lynne. The Bond: The Power of Connection . Hay House. ISBN 978-1-84850-478-3

108 https://www.nature.com/news/2009/090122/full/news.2009.50.html Nature international weekly journal of science: Atom takes a quantum leap

109 Joint quantum institute https://jqi.umd.edu/news/ first-teleportation-between-distant-atoms

110 https://www.youtube.com/watch?v=LjGgzxtxVXo University of Maryland, researchers make a teleportation breakthrough!

111 Source :: The Secrets Of Quantum Physics: Let There Be Life https://youtu.be/q4ONRJ1kTdA

112 McTaggart, Lynne. The Bond: The Power of Connection. Hay House.

113 Popp FA, Nagl W, Li KH, Scholz W, Weingartner O, Wolf R, Biophoton emission. New evidence for coherence and DNA as source, Cell Biophys 6:33–52, 1984.

114 S. Cohen and F. A. Popp, "Biophoton Emission of the Human Body", Journal of Photochemistry and Photobiology 40 (1997): 187–9.

115 F. A. Popp et al., "Mechanism of Interaction between Electromagnetic Fields and Living Organisms", Science in China (Series C) 43, no. 5 (2000): 507–18.

Made in the USA
Coppell, TX
26 March 2023

14771896R00177